PROGRAMMING MICROCONTROLLERS WITH C

Build Embedded Systems Projects

THOMPSON CARTER

TABLE OF CONTENTS

Introduction

Programming Microcontrollers with C: Build Embedded Systems

Embedded systems are at the heart of modern technological innovations. From the smartphones in our pockets to the intelligent systems governing critical medical devices, automotive safety features, and industrial automation, embedded systems are everywhere. These compact, specialized computers are engineered to perform specific tasks within a larger system, often with real-time constraints and limited resources.

However, designing embedded systems requires a unique set of skills, as they combine aspects of hardware and software development in a way that differs from traditional programming. If you are an engineer, hobbyist, or developer interested in the exciting world of embedded systems, then this book, *Programming Microcontrollers with C: Build Embedded Systems*, is for you. It is designed to help you build practical embedded systems from scratch, using the C programming language—one of the most widely used and efficient languages for programming microcontrollers.

C is the language of choice for most embedded systems development due to its speed, efficiency, and level of control it offers over hardware. While higher-level languages may be used for more complex applications, C allows developers to work closely with the hardware, offering fine-tuned control over memory, processing power, and device peripherals. Whether you're building a simple LED blink program, developing a complex real-time control system, or integrating sensors for IoT applications, C remains a foundational tool in the embedded systems world.

Why This Book?

Embedded systems programming may seem daunting at first, especially when you encounter specialized terminology, hardware interfaces, and real-time constraints. But don't worry—this book is structured to break down these concepts into digestible chapters that will guide you from the very basics to more advanced topics, with a focus on practical, real-world examples.

What makes *Programming Microcontrollers with C* unique is its balance between theory and hands-on application. It emphasizes not just understanding the theory behind embedded systems but also gives you plenty of opportunities to build, test, and troubleshoot real embedded projects. By the end of the book, you will be able to design your own embedded systems, tackle hardware challenges, and develop embedded applications for a wide range of industries.

Who This Book Is For

This book is intended for engineers, hobbyists, and students who are eager to learn how to program microcontrollers and build embedded systems from scratch. Whether you are completely new to embedded systems or you have some experience but need a structured approach to learning C programming for microcontrollers, this book will provide you with the knowledge and practical skills to succeed.

What You Will Learn

In the chapters ahead, you will learn about:

- **Microcontroller Basics**: You'll begin with an understanding of microcontroller architecture, and you will set up your first development environment to begin writing code.

- **Embedded C Programming**: You will learn the basics of C programming, tailored specifically for embedded systems. This includes understanding memory management, handling hardware peripherals, and writing efficient code for resource-constrained systems.

- **Peripherals and Interfaces**: We dive deep into essential hardware interfacing techniques such as working with GPIOs, ADCs, PWM, and communication protocols like UART, SPI, and I2C. You'll learn to work with common sensors and actuators, and understand the interaction between software and hardware.

- **Timers, Interrupts, and Real-Time Systems**: You will master advanced features like timers, interrupts, and real-time control systems, which are critical for applications that require precise control, such as robotics and automotive systems.

- **Advanced Techniques**: We'll cover advanced techniques for optimizing code, using Real-Time Operating Systems (RTOS), and integrating wireless communication and Internet of Things (IoT) technologies into your embedded systems.

- **Debugging and Testing**: One of the most crucial skills for an embedded systems developer is debugging. You will learn how to troubleshoot your code, monitor hardware performance, and use specialized tools to find and fix issues in your embedded systems.

- **Practical Projects**: Throughout the book, you will work on real-world projects, from basic tasks like blinking LEDs and reading sensors to more complex tasks such as creating a cloud-connected IoT device or building a wireless sensor network.

By the end of this journey, you will be able to:

- Write efficient, well-optimized code for embedded microcontrollers.
- Interface and communicate with a wide range of sensors, actuators, and peripherals.
- Design and implement real-time embedded systems.
- Debug and troubleshoot embedded systems effectively.
- Integrate advanced features like wireless communication and IoT capabilities into your embedded projects.

The Structure of This Book

This book is divided into 25 chapters, each building upon the previous one, so you can progress from a beginner to an advanced level of expertise. Each chapter begins with foundational concepts, followed by practical, hands-on examples that you can replicate and modify to suit your needs. You will also encounter tips, best practices, and troubleshooting techniques to help you avoid common pitfalls in embedded development.

Why Embedded Systems?

Embedded systems have become an essential part of modern engineering, driving innovation in industries such as automation, automotive, healthcare, telecommunications, consumer electronics, and aerospace. The need for highly efficient, low-power, and reliable devices has only increased as more devices become interconnected through the Internet of Things (IoT).

As embedded systems become more sophisticated, developers are required to write efficient, high-performance software that interacts with the underlying hardware and meets real-time requirements. This presents both a challenge and an opportunity. By learning how to program microcontrollers in C, you are gaining the ability to design solutions for this rapidly growing and highly rewarding field.

Final Thoughts

Whether you're looking to develop embedded systems for industrial automation, medical devices, or consumer products, *Programming Microcontrollers with C: Build Embedded Systems* will give you the skills, knowledge, and confidence to build your own embedded applications. This book is your starting point for developing powerful, efficient, and real-time embedded systems that make a difference in the world around you.

Let's dive in and start building embedded systems with C!

Chapter 1: Introduction to Embedded Systems and Microcontrollers

What Are Embedded Systems?

Understanding Embedded Systems and Their Significance in Daily   Life

An embedded system is a specialized computer system designed to perform dedicated functions or tasks within a larger system. Unlike general-purpose computers, embedded systems are designed for specific applications, often with real-time computing constraints. They are typically optimized for efficiency, power consumption, and reliability.

Embedded systems are everywhere. Some examples include:

- **Consumer Electronics**: Microcontrollers control functions in devices such as microwaves, washing machines, refrigerators, and smart TVs. These systems handle user inputs, control motors, sensors, and provide interactive feedback through displays.
- **Automotive**: In modern vehicles, embedded systems monitor sensors, manage airbag deployment, control braking systems (ABS), and even power advanced driver-assistance systems (ADAS). For example, microcontrollers are at the heart of automatic climate control systems, engine control units (ECUs), and infotainment systems.

- **Medical Devices**: Embedded systems in medical devices manage critical tasks such as monitoring patient vitals, administering insulin pumps, and running MRI machines. The precision and reliability of these systems are crucial for patient safety.

- **Industrial Applications**: From controlling robots in factories to managing complex industrial processes, embedded systems ensure smooth operation and safety. Microcontrollers manage everything from assembly lines to packaging systems and even smart grid technologies.

These systems provide reliable, real-time processing, often in environments where power consumption and space are limited.

The Role of Microcontrollers in Embedded Systems

What Are Microcontrollers?
Microcontrollers are compact integrated circuits that contain a processor, memory, and input/output (I/O) peripherals, all embedded on a single chip. They are the "brains" of embedded systems, enabling interaction with sensors, motors, and other electronic devices. Microcontrollers are typically designed to be small, low-cost, and energy-efficient, making them perfect for embedded applications.

- **Difference from General-Purpose Processors**
General-purpose processors (CPUs) found in personal

computers or servers are designed to handle a wide variety of tasks and support large operating systems like Windows or Linux. In contrast, microcontrollers are optimized for specific tasks and operate with minimal resources. While CPUs may have a large amount of RAM, storage, and processing power, microcontrollers typically operate with limited resources (RAM, ROM, and processing speed).

- **Examples of Popular Microcontrollers**
  - o **ARM**: ARM processors are widely used in embedded systems due to their low power consumption, high performance, and scalability. Examples include the STM32 family of microcontrollers, which are popular for a range of applications, from consumer electronics to industrial automation.
  - o **AVR**: AVR microcontrollers (e.g., ATmega328) are well-known for their use in Arduino development boards. These microcontrollers are favored for their simplicity, low cost, and ease of use in hobbyist projects and educational settings.
  - o **PIC**: PIC microcontrollers, developed by Microchip Technology, are used in everything from automotive applications to home appliances. Known for their versatility and low power consumption, they are found in many embedded applications.

- o **ESP32**: A powerful microcontroller often used in IoT (Internet of Things) projects, the ESP32 features both Wi-Fi and Bluetooth capabilities, making it ideal for connected devices.

Overview of C for Microcontroller Programming

Why C is the Language of Choice for Embedded Systems

C is the dominant programming language for embedded systems, and for good reason:

- **Efficiency**: C allows for low-level access to memory and hardware, which is essential in embedded systems where every byte of memory and clock cycle counts. This efficiency makes C suitable for resource-constrained environments.

- **Portability**: C code can be compiled for various microcontroller architectures, making it possible to use the same codebase across different hardware platforms.

- **Control Over Hardware**: C allows direct manipulation of hardware resources such as memory, I/O ports, and registers, giving developers full control over how the embedded system operates. This is crucial in embedded systems, where precise hardware control is required.

- **Wide Support**: Most embedded toolchains, IDEs, and compilers are designed to work with C, making it the language of choice for engineers and developers in the embedded space.

Basic Syntax and Structure
C programming for embedded systems follows the same basic syntax as C for general-purpose computing. Key features include:

- **Variables and Data Types**: C provides fundamental data types like int, char, and float, as well as structures and arrays for organizing data.
- **Control Flow**: C uses common control flow structures such as if, else, while, and for loops, which are vital for implementing logic and decision-making in embedded systems.
- **Functions**: Functions in C are used to structure code logically, helping to break complex tasks into manageable pieces.

Although C is a high-level language, it allows for low-level access to hardware, which is essential for embedded systems programming.

Setting Up Your Development Environment
Installing Tools Like IDEs and Toolchains
The development environment for microcontroller programming typically includes a set of tools and libraries for writing, compiling, and debugging code. Some of the most commonly used tools are:

- **Integrated Development Environments (IDEs)**: These provide a user-friendly interface for writing code, compiling, and debugging. Examples include:
  - **MPLAB X**: The IDE for PIC microcontrollers from Microchip. It provides an integrated environment for development, debugging, and programming.
  - **Keil uVision**: A popular IDE for ARM-based microcontrollers. It supports a wide range of hardware and is often used in professional embedded development.
  - **Arduino IDE**: A beginner-friendly IDE for programming AVR-based microcontrollers like the ATmega328, often used in hobbyist and educational applications.
- **Compilers**: Toolchains such as GCC (GNU Compiler Collection) are used to compile C code into machine-readable code that can run on microcontrollers. Each microcontroller family typically has its own set of compilers.

Setting Up Hardware for Microcontroller Programming
Once your development environment is set up, you will need to configure the hardware for programming. This often involves:

- **Connecting a Development Board**: Most microcontroller manufacturers offer development boards (e.g., Arduino,

STM32 Nucleo, ESP32 DevKit) that allow for easy programming and debugging.

- **Programming Interface**: Many microcontrollers require a programmer or debugger to load the code onto the chip. For example, you might use an **Arduino USB cable** to upload code to an Arduino board, or a **JTAG/SWD interface** to program more advanced microcontrollers like STM32.

Setting up the development environment and hardware will be your first step toward creating functional embedded systems with C programming.

This chapter provides the foundational knowledge necessary for diving into embedded systems and programming microcontrollers using C. The next chapters will build on this knowledge and guide you through the process of designing and developing embedded systems, from simple tasks like controlling LEDs to more complex systems like sensor integration and wireless communication.

Chapter 2: The Basics of C Programming

C Syntax Refresher

Variables, Data Types, Operators, and Control Structures in C

Before diving into programming embedded systems, it's essential to refresh the basic elements of the C programming language, which serves as the foundation for writing code on microcontrollers.

- **Variables and Data Types**: In C, variables are used to store data. Each variable is associated with a data type that determines the kind of value it can hold. Common data types in C include:
  - **int**: Integer values, typically 16, 32, or 64 bits in size.
  - **float**: Floating-point numbers, used to represent decimals.
  - **char**: Used for single characters, stored as ASCII values.
  - **unsigned**: Used to store only non-negative values.
  - **long, short**: Variants of integers with different sizes.
- **Operators**: C provides a range of operators for performing operations on variables. These include:
  - **Arithmetic operators**: +, -, *, /, %
  - **Relational operators**: ==, !=, <, >, <=, >=
  - **Logical operators**: &&, ||, !

- o **Bitwise operators**: &, |, ^, ~, <<, >>
- o **Assignment operators**: =, +=, -=, *=, /=
- o **Increment and Decrement**: ++, --

- **Control Structures**: Control flow structures allow you to dictate the flow of the program. Common structures include:
  - o **If-Else Statements**: Conditional statements to execute code based on a condition.

    c

    ```
    if (x > 0) {
        // Do something
    } else {
        // Do something else
    }
    ```

  - o **Switch-Case Statements**: Alternative to multiple if-else conditions, useful when dealing with discrete values.

    c

    ```
    switch (variable) {
        case 1:
            // Code for case 1
            break;
        case 2:
            // Code for case 2
            break;
    ```

```
default:
    // Code for other cases
    break;
}
```

- o **Loops**: Loops allow repetitive execution of code. Two main types of loops in C are:
    - **For Loop**: Used when the number of iterations is known beforehand.

    c

    ```
    for (int i = 0; i < 10; i++) {
        // Code to execute
    }
    ```

    - **While Loop**: Used when the number of iterations is unknown, and the loop continues until a condition is false.

    c

    ```
    while (condition) {
        // Code to execute
    }
    ```

    - **Do-While Loop**: Similar to the while loop, but ensures the code runs at least once.

    c

```
do {
    // Code to execute
} while (condition);
```

Functions and Program Flow

Writing Functions, Passing Arguments, and Returning Values´

Functions are fundamental in C programming as they allow you to break down tasks into reusable blocks of code. Functions can accept inputs (parameters) and return outputs (values).

- **Function Definition**: A function is defined by specifying its return type, name, and parameters.

  c

  ```
  int add(int a, int b) {
      return a + b;
  }
  ```

- **Function Call**: To use a function, you call it in your code, passing the necessary arguments.

  c

  ```
  int result = add(5, 3);  // result will be 8
  ```

Program   **Flow**

The flow of a C program depends on how the functions and control

structures are organized. The execution starts from the main()
function, which is the entry point of the program.

c

```c
#include <stdio.h>

int main() {
    int x = 5;
    int y = 3;
    int sum = add(x, y);  // Call to the add function
    printf("The sum is: %d\n", sum);
    return 0;
}
```

Memory Management

Understanding Stack vs. Heap, Pointers, and Memory Allocation

One of the key differences between embedded systems
programming and general-purpose application programming is the
need to understand memory management. Efficient memory usage
is critical when working with microcontrollers, which often have
limited memory resources.

- **Stack Memory**: The stack is used to store local variables
  and function call information. It is managed automatically,

with memory being allocated and deallocated when functions are called and return.

- ○ **Function call stack**: Each time a function is called, the return address, local variables, and function parameters are pushed onto the stack.

- **Heap Memory**: The heap is used for dynamic memory allocation. When you need memory that is not automatically deallocated when a function exits, you can allocate memory on the heap using malloc() or calloc() and free it with free().

c

```
int *ptr = (int*) malloc(sizeof(int));   // Allocating memory for an integer
*ptr = 10;
free(ptr);  // Releasing the memory
```

- **Pointers**: A pointer is a variable that stores the memory address of another variable. Pointers are extremely useful for manipulating data in memory directly, which is often required in embedded systems for accessing hardware or memory-mapped registers.

- ○ **Dereferencing a pointer** allows you to access the value stored at the memory address the pointer points to.

c

```
int x = 10;
int *ptr = &x;  // ptr now holds the address of x
printf("%d", *ptr);  // Dereferencing the pointer to print the value of x
```

By understanding how stack and heap memory work, and using pointers to manipulate data, engineers can optimize their embedded programs to make efficient use of the available memory and resources on microcontrollers.

This chapter serves as a fundamental refresher on C programming concepts, ensuring you are comfortable with basic syntax and memory management before diving deeper into the embedded world. The examples provided will help you get hands-on experience with the C language, laying the groundwork for more complex projects involving microcontrollers.

Chapter 3: Microcontroller Architecture and Features

Understanding the Microcontroller's Internal Architecture

Microcontrollers are the heart of embedded systems, combining a CPU, memory, and peripheral components on a single chip. Understanding the architecture of microcontrollers is essential for effective programming, as it allows developers to interact directly with the hardware, optimizing performance and resource usage. In this section, we'll break down the components that make up a microcontroller and explore the architectures of popular microcontrollers.

- **CPU (Central Processing Unit)**: The CPU executes instructions from your program. It is responsible for processing data, running computations, and controlling the entire system. The CPU's speed, measured in MHz or GHz, determines how quickly it can execute tasks.

- **Memory**: Microcontrollers typically contain several types of memory, each with a specific function:

  - **Flash Memory**: This is non-volatile memory used to store the program code. Unlike RAM, flash memory retains data even when power is turned off.

  - **RAM (Random Access Memory)**: This volatile memory is used to store data during program execution. When power is lost, data in RAM is erased.

- o **EEPROM (Electrically Erasable Programmable Read-Only Memory)**: This non-volatile memory is used for storing configuration settings or data that needs to persist across resets.

- **Peripherals**: Microcontrollers come with built-in peripherals that extend their functionality. Common peripherals include:

  - o **Timers**: Used for generating precise delays or measuring intervals.

  - o **ADC/DAC (Analog-to-Digital/Digital-to-Analog Converters)**: Allow microcontrollers to interact with analog signals, converting them to digital values (ADC) or vice versa (DAC).

  - o **Communication Interfaces**: Such as UART, SPI, I2C, which allow the microcontroller to communicate with other devices, sensors, or actuators.

Common Microcontroller Architectures:

1. **ARM   Cortex-M**:

   The ARM Cortex-M series is one of the most popular microcontroller families. These microcontrollers are known for their low power consumption and high performance, making them ideal for a variety of applications, from consumer electronics to industrial automation. The architecture is highly scalable, with different cores such as Cortex-M0, M3, M4, and M7 catering to various needs in terms of processing power and functionality.

2. **AVR**:

   AVR microcontrollers, developed by Atmel (now part of Microchip), are widely used in hobbyist projects and early microcontroller-based platforms like Arduino. They feature an 8-bit architecture, but newer AVR chips can be 32-bit. AVR microcontrollers are simple to program and have a rich set of peripherals.

3. **PIC**:

   PIC microcontrollers, developed by Microchip Technology, are known for their simplicity and reliability. They are available in a wide range of options, from 8-bit to 32-bit processors. PIC microcontrollers are commonly used in industrial applications due to their low cost and extensive peripheral support.

Understanding the Clock and Timing

The clock is an essential component of microcontroller operation, governing the timing of all internal processes. The clock ensures synchronization across different parts of the microcontroller, enabling orderly execution of instructions and precise control over hardware peripherals.

- **Role of the Clock**:
  - o Every microcontroller has a **system clock**, which determines how quickly it can process instructions. The clock speed is usually expressed in MHz (megahertz) or GHz (gigahertz), indicating how many millions or billions of cycles it can execute per second.
  - o The clock is also responsible for timing the operation of peripherals like **timers**, **serial communication interfaces**, and **PWM (pulse-width modulation)** signals. A high clock speed allows for faster execution, but it also leads to higher power consumption, so designers often choose a clock frequency that balances performance and energy efficiency.
- **Setting Up Timers for Delays and Precise Measurements**:
  - o **Timers** are critical for managing timing-related tasks, such as generating precise delays or measuring the time between events. For example, if you want to blink an LED every second, you can use a timer to generate an interrupt at 1-second

intervals, at which point the microcontroller can toggle the LED.

- o **Prescaling**: Timers often come with prescalers that allow you to scale the timer frequency. For instance, if your microcontroller's clock runs at 16 MHz but you want to measure events at a slower rate (e.g., every 1 ms), you can use a prescaler to reduce the timer's frequency.

Digital I/O Basics

At the core of microcontroller functionality is the ability to interact with the external world. This is achieved through **digital I/O** (input/output) pins, which are used to read signals from sensors (input) or control external devices (output).

- **GPIO Pins (General Purpose Input/Output)**:
  - o Most microcontrollers come with multiple GPIO pins that can be configured either as inputs or outputs. Each pin can be set to **high** or **low** (1 or 0), and its behavior can be controlled through registers in the microcontroller's memory.
  - o **Input**: When a GPIO pin is configured as an input, it can be used to read signals from external sources.

For example, it could read the state of a button or sensor.

- ○ **Output**: When a GPIO pin is configured as an output, it can be used to drive external devices. For example, it could control an LED, relay, or motor.

- **Configuring GPIO Pins**:
  - ○ Microcontroller IDEs or programming environments usually provide built-in libraries or functions to set up GPIO pins. For example, in the Arduino IDE, the function pinMode(pin, INPUT) configures a pin as an input, while pinMode(pin, OUTPUT) sets it as an output.
  - ○ **Reading Input**: Once configured as an input, you can read the value of a GPIO pin using functions like digitalRead(pin), which returns either HIGH (1) or LOW (0) based on the pin's voltage level.
  - ○ **Writing Output**: For writing to a pin, functions like digitalWrite(pin, HIGH) or digitalWrite(pin, LOW) can be used to set the voltage level on the pin.

Real-World   **Example**:
To better understand GPIO functionality, let's look at an example of turning an LED on and off based on a button press:

1. Set one pin as an input for the button and another pin as an output for the LED.

2. The program continuously checks the button's state using digitalRead() on the input pin.

3. If the button is pressed (input is HIGH), the program uses digitalWrite() to turn on the LED.

4. If the button is released (input is LOW), the LED is turned off.

c

```c
#define BUTTON_PIN 2
#define LED_PIN 13

void setup() {
  pinMode(BUTTON_PIN, INPUT);
  pinMode(LED_PIN, OUTPUT);
}

void loop() {
  int buttonState = digitalRead(BUTTON_PIN);
  if (buttonState == HIGH) {
   digitalWrite(LED_PIN, HIGH);  // Turn on LED
  } else {
   digitalWrite(LED_PIN, LOW);   // Turn off LED
  }
}
```

In this example, when the button is pressed, the GPIO pin connected to the LED is set to HIGH, turning the LED on. If the button is released, the LED is turned off by setting the pin to LOW.

In this chapter, we've explored the fundamental concepts of microcontroller architecture, including memory, peripherals, and the clock system, as well as basic I/O operations using GPIO pins. Understanding these components is crucial for efficient microcontroller programming and will lay the groundwork for more advanced projects in subsequent chapters.

Chapter 4: Interfacing with Peripherals: LEDs, Buttons, and Switches

Using GPIO Pins for LEDs and Buttons

In embedded systems, **General Purpose Input/Output (GPIO)** pins are the primary method of interacting with external devices. These pins can be configured as either inputs or outputs, allowing you to interface with various peripherals, such as LEDs, buttons, and switches. Understanding how to use GPIO pins efficiently is crucial for building functional embedded systems.

- **LEDs (Light Emitting Diodes)** are one of the most common output devices used in embedded systems. By controlling the voltage sent to an LED, you can turn it on, off, or make it blink. This process is done using a GPIO pin configured as an output.

  - **Basic LED Blink Program**: The simplest LED interface is to blink an LED on and off at regular intervals. This requires writing a program that toggles the GPIO pin at a specified frequency (e.g., every 500ms).

    c

    #define LED_PIN 13 // Define GPIO pin for LED

```
void setup() {
  pinMode(LED_PIN, OUTPUT); // Set the LED_PIN as output
}

void loop() {
  digitalWrite(LED_PIN, HIGH); // Turn the LED on
  delay(500);                  // Wait for 500ms
  digitalWrite(LED_PIN, LOW);  // Turn the LED off
  delay(500);                  // Wait for 500ms
}
```

In this simple program:

- pinMode() is used to set the pin mode (output for the LED).
- digitalWrite() is used to turn the LED on (HIGH) or off (LOW).
- delay() provides the timing for the blink.

- **Debouncing Buttons**: Buttons are a common input device used in embedded systems, but when you press a button, the signal can be noisy. This is known as **contact bounce**. To handle this, a technique called **debouncing** is used to ensure that only a single signal is read when the button is pressed or released.

  o **Button Debouncing Method**: This method involves checking the state of the button at intervals to ensure that the state is stable. Typically, a delay of 10-50 milliseconds is added after each button press to avoid multiple readings from a single press.

c

```c
#define BUTTON_PIN 2  // Define GPIO pin for button
#define LED_PIN 13    // Define GPIO pin for LED

void setup() {
  pinMode(BUTTON_PIN, INPUT);  // Set the button pin as input
  pinMode(LED_PIN, OUTPUT);    // Set the LED pin as output
}

void loop() {
  int buttonState = digitalRead(BUTTON_PIN);  // Read the button state

  if (buttonState == HIGH) { // If button is pressed
    digitalWrite(LED_PIN, HIGH); // Turn LED on
  } else {
    digitalWrite(LED_PIN, LOW);  // Turn LED off
  }

  delay(50); // Debounce delay to avoid multiple reads
}
```

- **Key Concepts**:
  - digitalRead() is used to read the state of the button.

- The delay() function introduces a small wait between button presses to allow for debouncing.

Real-World Example: Building a Basic LED Flasher and Button-Controlled LED Program

In this real-world example, we'll create a program that combines both an LED and a button. The program will make the LED blink at regular intervals, and when the button is pressed, the LED will stay on.

1. **Hardware Setup**:
   o Connect an LED to pin 13 (or another GPIO pin) with a current-limiting resistor.
   o Connect a pushbutton to pin 2 (or another GPIO pin) and use a pull-down resistor to ensure a stable low signal when the button is not pressed.
2. **Program Explanation**:
   o The LED will blink in the loop() function, but when the button is pressed, the LED will turn on and stay on, overriding the blinking behavior.
   o This is a simple, yet effective demonstration of how to use input (button) and output (LED) with GPIO pins.

c

```
#define BUTTON_PIN 2  // Define GPIO pin for button
#define LED_PIN 13    // Define GPIO pin for LED

void setup() {
  pinMode(BUTTON_PIN, INPUT);  // Set button pin as input
  pinMode(LED_PIN, OUTPUT);    // Set LED pin as output
}

void loop() {
  int buttonState = digitalRead(BUTTON_PIN);  // Read the button state

  if (buttonState == HIGH) {  // If button is pressed
    digitalWrite(LED_PIN, HIGH);  // Turn the LED on
  } else {  // If button is not pressed
    digitalWrite(LED_PIN, LOW);   // Turn the LED off
  }

  delay(200);  // Small delay to make the LED state change visible
}
```

Key Takeaways

- **GPIO Pins**: They are the primary means of interacting with external devices like LEDs and buttons.
- **LEDs**: Controlled by setting GPIO pins to either HIGH (on) or LOW (off), with delays to create blinking effects.

- **Buttons**: Require debouncing to prevent false triggering due to contact bounce. This is accomplished by checking the state of the button after a small delay.

- **Practical Example**: A simple program to blink an LED and control its state with a button, showcasing input-output interactions in embedded systems.

This chapter provides you with foundational knowledge of working with GPIO pins, a key aspect of microcontroller programming. These skills are essential for developing interactive systems, such as simple user interfaces in embedded applications, control systems, or sensor-based designs.

Chapter 5: Analog Signals and ADCs

What is Analog-to-Digital Conversion (ADC)?

Embedded systems often need to interact with the physical world, and many sensors or devices produce **analog signals** (e.g., temperature sensors, light sensors, or microphones). Microcontrollers typically work with **digital signals**, so converting these analog signals into a digital format that the microcontroller can understand is essential. This process is known as **Analog-to-Digital Conversion (ADC)**.

- **Analog Signals**: Analog signals are continuous and vary over time, typically representing real-world physical phenomena like temperature, pressure, light intensity, or sound. For example, a temperature sensor might produce a voltage that varies from 0V to 3.3V depending on the temperature.

- **Digital Signals**: Digital signals, on the other hand, are discrete and have values that are represented as binary numbers (0s and 1s). The microcontroller processes data in digital form, so it must convert the incoming analog signal to a digital value that can be interpreted and used by the program.

- **ADC Process**:
    - **Sampling**: The ADC samples the analog signal at regular intervals (usually many times per second).

The more frequent the sampling, the more accurately it captures the variations of the analog signal.

○ **Resolution**: The resolution of an ADC is defined by the number of bits in its output. A **10-bit ADC**, for example, can output values from 0 to 1023, representing 1024 distinct levels of the input signal. Higher resolution means more precise measurements.

In microcontrollers, the ADC converts the input voltage into a digital number that corresponds to a value within the ADC's voltage reference range. The higher the resolution of the ADC, the more granular the digital representation of the analog signal.

Using the ADC in C

Once you understand the basic concepts of ADCs, it's time to interface with them in your microcontroller code. Let's walk through how to configure and use an ADC in C.

1. **Configuring the ADC**:
   ○ Before reading from the ADC, it must be configured to operate in the desired mode. This typically includes setting the **ADC reference voltage**, selecting the **ADC input channel** (the

analog pin to read from), and specifying the **ADC clock**.

- ○ The ADC can be configured to either run in **single-ended** mode (where one channel is read at a time) or **differential** mode (where two input channels are compared).

2. **Starting the ADC Conversion**:

- ○ Most microcontrollers initiate an ADC conversion by setting a specific bit in a control register. The ADC starts converting the input signal, and the microcontroller can continue other tasks while waiting for the conversion to complete.
- ○ Once the conversion is complete, the result is available in a register, and it can be read by the program.

3. **Reading the ADC Result**:

- ○ The result of the ADC conversion is stored as a digital value, usually in a specific register. You can then read this value and process it to interpret the measured signal (e.g., temperature, light intensity).
- ○ If the ADC has a lower resolution (e.g., 8-bit), you'll need to account for the scaling when using the result.

Real-World Example: Reading a Temperature Sensor's Analog Output

Let's apply what we've learned to a practical example. We will read the analog output from a temperature sensor (e.g., an LM35) and convert it to a temperature value.

Hardware Setup:

- **Temperature Sensor**: An LM35 temperature sensor produces an analog voltage that is directly proportional to the temperature in degrees Celsius. The output voltage increases by 10mV for every degree Celsius. For example, a temperature of 25°C will produce 250mV, and 30°C will produce 300mV.

- **Microcontroller**: Let's assume we're using an Arduino-based microcontroller (e.g., an ATmega328P) for this example, but this can be applied to many other microcontrollers as well.

Step-by-Step Implementation:

1. **Configure the ADC**: First, you need to configure the ADC in your microcontroller. This includes selecting the input channel connected to the temperature sensor and setting up the reference voltage.

2. **Start the ADC Conversion**: To start the ADC conversion, set the appropriate bits in the control registers. This tells the microcontroller to sample the voltage on the analog input pin connected to the LM35.

3. **Read the ADC Value**: Once the conversion is complete, the ADC value will be available in a register. Since the ADC resolution is typically 10-bits on most microcontrollers, the value will range from 0 to 1023.

4. **Convert the ADC Value to Temperature**: The ADC result must be converted to a real-world temperature value. This requires some simple math:

    o Assume the reference voltage is 5V, and the sensor outputs 10mV per degree Celsius.

    o The ADC value can be mapped to a voltage by dividing the ADC result by 1023 (the maximum ADC value) and multiplying by the reference voltage (e.g., 5V).

    o Then, convert the voltage to a temperature value by dividing by 10mV per degree.

Example Code (Arduino):

c

```
// Define the ADC channel (e.g., A0 for analog input pin A0)
#define TEMP_SENSOR_PIN A0

void setup() {
  // Initialize serial communication for debugging
  Serial.begin(9600);
}
```

```
void loop() {
  // Read the analog value from the temperature sensor
  int adcValue = analogRead(TEMP_SENSOR_PIN);

  // Convert the ADC value to voltage (assuming 5V reference)
  float voltage = adcValue * (5.0 / 1023.0);

  // Convert the voltage to temperature (LM35: 10mV per degree)
  float temperatureC = voltage * 100.0;

  // Print the temperature to the serial monitor
  Serial.print("Temperature: ");
  Serial.print(temperatureC);
  Serial.println(" C");

  // Wait for a short time before reading again
  delay(1000);
}
```

Explanation of the Code:

1. **analogRead(TEMP_SENSOR_PIN)**: Reads the analog value from the sensor connected to the specified input pin.

2. **Voltage Calculation**: The ADC value is mapped to the actual voltage by dividing the ADC result by 1023 (the maximum ADC value) and multiplying by 5V (the reference voltage).

3. **Temperature Calculation**: The voltage is multiplied by 100 to convert the voltage (in volts) to temperature in Celsius (since the LM35 outputs 10mV per degree).

4. **Serial Output**: The temperature is displayed on the serial monitor for easy monitoring.

:

In this chapter, we learned how microcontrollers interact with analog sensors through **Analog-to-Digital Conversion (ADC)**. We discussed how to configure and use the ADC in C, and we worked through a practical example of reading a temperature sensor's analog output. By understanding ADCs and how to read analog signals, you can begin integrating real-world sensors into your embedded systems and making your microcontroller-based projects more interactive and responsive.

Chapter 6: Using Timers and Counters

Timers and Counters in Microcontrollers

Timers and counters are essential components of microcontrollers, providing the ability to measure time, generate periodic signals, and respond to specific intervals. Understanding how to use timers and counters is crucial for developing reliable and efficient embedded systems.

- **Timers**: A timer is a hardware module in a microcontroller that counts clock pulses (or oscillations from an internal clock source) at a specific frequency. It can be used to generate precise time delays, create periodic interrupts, and perform time-based tasks. Timers in microcontrollers typically allow for configurations such as setting an initial count value, defining overflow conditions, and generating interrupts after a certain period.

- **Counters**: A counter is similar to a timer, but instead of counting clock pulses, it counts external events, such as the number of pulses on a specific pin (e.g., from a sensor or external signal). Counters are ideal for measuring frequency, counting events, or triggering actions after a specific number of events have occurred.

Using Timers to Create Precise Time Delays

Microcontrollers generally operate with an internal clock, and timers use this clock to generate predictable time delays. These delays can be crucial for applications like creating periodic interrupts, controlling the timing of sensors, or managing communication protocols (e.g., SPI, UART).

1. **Configuring the Timer**:
   o Most microcontrollers have several timers that can be configured with different prescalers (which divide the clock speed) to adjust the timer's resolution.
   o For example, on an **Arduino** or **AVR** microcontroller, you can set up Timer1 (a 16-bit timer) to generate an interrupt every 1 millisecond.

2. **Setting Up Timer Interrupts**:
   o Interrupts are one of the most powerful features of microcontroller timers. When the timer overflows (or reaches a defined value), it can trigger an interrupt. This interrupt allows the program to perform a task (such as updating an LED or reading a sensor) without needing to constantly poll the timer.
   o For instance, if you wanted an LED to blink every 500 milliseconds, you could set up a timer interrupt to toggle the LED on or off at each timer overflow.

Counting Events and Pulses Using Timers

Timers can also be used to count external events, such as pulses on a GPIO pin or frequency of a signal. This can be very useful in applications where you need to count the number of occurrences of a physical event, like measuring the speed of a rotating wheel or detecting pulses from a sensor.

1. **Example of Pulse Counting**:
    - By configuring a timer to capture the number of rising or falling edges on an external pin, the microcontroller can count the number of pulses and calculate the frequency of an external signal.
    - For instance, counting the number of pulses from a tachometer or a rotary encoder can be used to measure the speed of a motor.

Real-World Example: Creating a Time-Based Interrupt to Blink an LED at a Fixed Rate

In this example, we will demonstrate how to use a timer to generate a fixed-rate interrupt that will blink an LED at a regular interval (e.g., every 500 milliseconds). The idea here is to configure a timer to overflow after 500 milliseconds, triggering an interrupt that toggles the state of an LED.

Example Code for Arduino (AVR):

c

```
// Define the pin for the LED
#define LED_PIN 13

void setup() {
  // Set LED_PIN as output
  pinMode(LED_PIN, OUTPUT);

  // Set up Timer1 to generate an interrupt every 500 milliseconds
  // Configure the timer for CTC (Clear Timer on Compare Match) mode
  TCCR1A = 0;  // Normal operation
  TCCR1B = (1 << WGM12) | (1 << CS12);  // CTC mode, prescaler = 256
  OCR1A = 6249;  // Set value to overflow every 500ms (16MHz clock)
  TIMSK1 |= (1 << OCIE1A);  // Enable Timer1 compare interrupt
}

void loop() {
  // Main loop does nothing, waiting for the interrupt
}

// Interrupt Service Routine (ISR) for Timer1 compare match
ISR(TIMER1_COMPA_vect) {
  // Toggle LED on pin 13
  digitalWrite(LED_PIN, !digitalRead(LED_PIN));
}
```

Explanation:

1. **Timer Configuration**:

o Timer1 is set to operate in CTC mode, where it counts up to a value stored in the **OCR1A** register. When the timer reaches this value, it resets and generates an interrupt.

o The prescaler is set to 256, which means the timer will count slower than the system clock. With a 16 MHz clock, this results in a timer overflow every 500 milliseconds (6250 counts).

2. **Interrupt Handling**:

o The **ISR(TIMER1_COMPA_vect)** function is executed when the timer overflows. This is where the LED state is toggled.

3. **Blinking the LED**:

o When the interrupt triggers, the ISR toggles the LED on pin 13, causing it to blink every 500 milliseconds.

Timers and counters are indispensable tools in embedded systems programming. By understanding how to configure and use timers, you can create precise time delays, manage periodic tasks, and measure external events. In this chapter, we learned how to set up a timer, generate interrupts, and use timers for counting external events. The real-world example of blinking an LED at fixed intervals demonstrated the application of timers for time-based control, a common requirement in embedded system design.

In the next chapter, we will explore **PWM (Pulse Width Modulation)**, a technique that uses timers to control the power delivered to devices such as motors, LEDs, and heating elements.

Chapter 7: Interrupts and Real-Time Systems

Understanding Interrupts

In embedded systems, **interrupts** are used to handle time-sensitive tasks efficiently without constantly checking (polling) for specific events. An interrupt is a mechanism that temporarily halts the normal execution of the program and allows the microcontroller to handle a specific event or condition. After the interrupt service routine (ISR) finishes, the program resumes execution from where it left off. Interrupts are essential for real-time systems where immediate responses to events are critical.

- **Polling vs. Interrupts**
    - **Polling**: Polling involves checking a condition or input repeatedly at regular intervals to detect if a specific event has occurred. For example, you might continuously check if a button is pressed by using a loop. While polling is simple to implement, it can be inefficient because the microcontroller spends a lot of time checking for events, even when there is no event happening.
    - **Interrupt-driven Systems**: Interrupts allow the microcontroller to "stop" the normal execution of the program to respond to an event when it occurs.

This eliminates the need for polling, allowing the system to perform other tasks while waiting for specific events.

Setting Up Interrupts in C

Microcontrollers generally have dedicated registers to enable interrupts, define which events trigger them, and specify the routines that should execute when an interrupt occurs. Setting up interrupts involves several key steps:

1. **Enable Global Interrupts**: Interrupts must be globally enabled, meaning the microcontroller needs to allow interrupt requests to be processed.

2. **Configure Specific Interrupts**: Each interrupt source (e.g., a button press, a timer overflow, or an external signal) has its own interrupt vector. You need to configure the microcontroller to listen for specific events on these pins or peripherals.

3. **Write the Interrupt Service Routine (ISR)**: This is the function that gets executed when an interrupt occurs. The ISR should be short and fast to prevent blocking other important tasks.

4. **Clear Interrupt Flags**: Once the ISR has executed, any flags indicating that the interrupt has occurred need to be cleared to allow for the next interrupt.

Here's a basic example in C to demonstrate setting up a simple interrupt for a button press:

c

```c
#include <avr/io.h>
#include <avr/interrupt.h>

void init_interrupt() {
    // Configure pin as input
    DDRD &= ~(1 << PD2); // Set PD2 as input (button)

    // Enable external interrupt on INT0 (button press)
    EIMSK |= (1 << INT0);   // Enable INT0 interrupt
    EICRA |= (1 << ISC01);   // Trigger on falling edge (button press)

    // Enable global interrupts
    sei();
}

ISR(INT0_vect) {
    // Interrupt Service Routine: Code to handle button press
    PORTB ^= (1 << PB0); // Toggle LED on PB0 when button is pressed
}

int main(void) {
    // Configure LED pin as output
    DDRB |= (1 << PB0);

    // Initialize interrupt
```

```
init_interrupt();

while(1) {
    // Main loop: microcontroller continues running other tasks
    // LED toggles whenever the button is pressed due to interrupt
}
}
```

In this example:

- The button is connected to pin **PD2** (INT0) and triggers an interrupt when pressed (falling edge).
- The ISR toggles an LED on pin **PB0** whenever the interrupt occurs.
- The sei() function enables global interrupts, allowing the microcontroller to respond to events.

Real-World Example: Implementing a Button Press Interrupt

In embedded systems, you often need to react to external events without constantly checking the state of inputs. A button press is a classic example of an event that can be handled by an interrupt, allowing the system to efficiently execute tasks only when needed.

- **Scenario**: Imagine designing a simple embedded system to control an LED with a button. Instead of constantly polling the button's state, the system can use an interrupt to trigger the LED's state change only when the button is pressed.

Steps:

1. Configure the button as an input pin.

2. Enable an external interrupt on the button pin.

3. Write an interrupt service routine that toggles the LED whenever the button is pressed.

4. Use a debouncing technique to ensure the button press is registered correctly, avoiding multiple triggers from a single press.

By using interrupts, this design allows the microcontroller to do other tasks while waiting for the button press, without the overhead of constant polling.

The Role of Interrupts in Real-Time Systems

In real-time systems, the timely execution of tasks is crucial. Interrupts are key to achieving real-time behavior in embedded systems. For example:

- In a **robotics system**, you may need to react to changes in sensor data (e.g., an object approaching the robot) within a specific time frame. Interrupts can be used to process sensor data immediately when it's available, without waiting for the main program to reach a specific point in its execution.

- In an **audio system**, real-time interrupts can handle tasks like generating sound waves or processing audio signals at a specific frequency.

Using interrupts in real-time systems ensures that critical tasks are executed immediately upon occurrence, without delay, and without continuously monitoring conditions. This results in a more efficient and responsive system.

Interrupts are fundamental in the design of embedded systems, providing a powerful mechanism to handle real-time events and reduce the need for constant polling. By understanding how to use interrupts, embedded systems can be made more efficient, responsive, and capable of handling multiple time-sensitive tasks simultaneously.

In this chapter, you've learned how interrupts work, how to configure them, and how to use them in C for real-world applications. The practical example of using a button press interrupt to toggle an LED demonstrates how interrupts can optimize system performance and enable real-time responses.

In the next chapter, we will dive into **real-time operating systems (RTOS)** and explore how these systems manage tasks and resources to ensure timely execution in more complex embedded applications.

Chapter 8: Communication Protocols: UART

Introduction to Serial Communication

Serial communication is a method used to transfer data one bit at a time, over a single communication line, making it ideal for embedded systems where resources like pins and bandwidth are limited. One of the most common forms of serial communication is **UART (Universal Asynchronous Receiver/Transmitter)**. It is used to transfer data between a microcontroller and peripheral devices (such as sensors, other microcontrollers, or a computer) using a standard set of protocols.

- **What is UART?** UART is a simple and efficient communication protocol that doesn't require a clock signal to synchronize the data transfer. It's asynchronous because the data is transmitted without the need for a shared clock between the transmitter and receiver. Instead, both devices agree on the speed of communication (baud rate), and each bit is transmitted sequentially. The UART communication consists of a series of frames that include a start bit, data bits, an optional parity bit, and one or more stop bits.

- **How UART Works** In UART communication, there are typically two main components:

1. **Transmitter**: This is the device or component that sends data. It takes a series of bits and sends them sequentially to the receiver.

2. **Receiver**: The receiver takes the serial data sent by the transmitter and converts it back into a form that can be used or processed.

Data is transmitted using the following components:

- **Start bit**: Indicates the beginning of a data frame.
- **Data bits**: Usually 8 bits, which represent the actual data being transmitted.
- **Parity bit** (optional): Used for error checking.
- **Stop bits**: Indicate the end of the data frame. One or two stop bits are typically used.

Programming UART for Communication

In embedded systems programming, UART is often used to communicate between a microcontroller and other systems, such as a computer or another microcontroller. Setting up UART involves configuring several parameters, including the baud rate, data bits, parity bits, and stop bits. These parameters must be consistent between both the sender and receiver devices for successful communication.

Key UART Parameters:

1. **Baud Rate**: The rate at which data is transmitted, typically measured in bits per second (bps). Common baud rates are 9600, 115200, etc. The baud rate on both ends must match for the data to be correctly interpreted.

2. **Data Bits**: Typically, 8 bits of data are transmitted in one frame, though 5, 6, or 7 bits may also be used in some applications.

3. **Parity Bits**: A parity bit is used for error detection, where an even or odd number of bits are used to check for errors in the data being transmitted. You can set the parity to none, even, or odd.

4. **Stop Bits**: Used to indicate the end of the transmission. Common values for stop bits are 1 or 2.

Steps to Configure UART on a Microcontroller:

1. **Initialize UART Communication**: The first step is to configure the UART peripheral on the microcontroller. This includes setting the baud rate, data bits, stop bits, and parity. Many microcontrollers provide functions to initialize UART communication, but the settings will depend on the specific hardware and the microcontroller's peripheral library.

2. **Transmit Data**: Once UART is initialized, the microcontroller can send data by loading the data into a

transmit register. The data is then shifted out serially over the TX pin.

3. **Receive Data**: On the receiver end, the microcontroller waits for incoming data and loads it into a receive register. The program will read this register to process the received data.

Here is an example of how UART might be configured and used in C for a microcontroller:

c

```c
#include <avr/io.h>

void UART_init(unsigned int baud) {
    // Set the baud rate
    unsigned int ubrr = F_CPU / 16 / baud - 1;
    UBRR0H = (unsigned char)(ubrr >> 8);
    UBRR0L = (unsigned char)ubrr;

    // Enable receiver and transmitter
    UCSR0B = (1 << RXEN0) | (1 << TXEN0);

    // Set frame format: 8 data bits, no parity, 1 stop bit
    UCSR0C = (1 << UCSZ01) | (1 << UCSZ00);
}

void UART_transmit(unsigned char data) {
    // Wait for the transmit buffer to be empty
```

```
    while (!(UCSR0A & (1 << UDRE0))) ;

    // Put data into the buffer, which sends it
    UDR0 = data;
}

unsigned char UART_receive(void) {
    // Wait for data to be received
    while (!(UCSR0A & (1 << RXC0))) ;

    // Get and return the received data from the buffer
    return UDR0;
}

int main(void) {
    UART_init(9600);  // Initialize UART with a baud rate of 9600

    while (1) {
        unsigned char received_data = UART_receive(); // Receive data
        UART_transmit(received_data); // Echo received data back
    }

    return 0;
}
```

In this example:

- The UART_init() function sets up the baud rate, data bits, and other parameters.

- The UART_transmit() function sends data, while the UART_receive() function waits for incoming data and returns it.
- The main() function continuously receives data and echoes it back to the sender.

Real-World Example

Sending and Receiving Data Between a Microcontroller and a Computer via UART

Let's walk through a simple real-world example of using UART for communication between a microcontroller and a computer. In this scenario, the microcontroller will send a message to the computer, and the computer will respond by sending data back to the microcontroller.

Required Components:

1. Microcontroller (e.g., Arduino, STM32, or ESP32).
2. USB-to-serial adapter (if not using a built-in UART-to-USB bridge like in Arduino boards).
3. Computer with a serial terminal program (e.g., PuTTY, Tera Term, or minicom).

Steps:

1. **Set up the microcontroller's UART for communication.**

o Initialize UART with the correct baud rate (e.g., 9600), 8 data bits, no parity, and 1 stop bit.

2. **Write a program on the microcontroller to send data** (e.g., a simple "Hello, world!" message).

3. **Use a serial terminal on the computer to communicate with the microcontroller.**

   o The terminal will show the data sent by the microcontroller.

   o The computer can also send data back to the microcontroller.

For example, using the Arduino IDE, you can use the Serial.write() and Serial.read() functions to send and receive data. The following Arduino code sends a string and echoes back any received data:

cpp

```
void setup() {
  Serial.begin(9600); // Start UART communication at 9600 baud
}

void loop() {
  Serial.println("Hello, World!"); // Send message to the computer
  if (Serial.available()) {
    char receivedChar = Serial.read(); // Read the incoming byte
    Serial.print("Received: ");
    Serial.println(receivedChar); // Echo back the received byte
  }
```

```
delay(1000);  // Wait for a second before sending again
}
```

This simple example shows how UART is used to exchange data between the microcontroller and the computer. You can extend this further to create complex communication protocols or send data between multiple devices using UART.

In this chapter, we have learned about **UART communication**, which is a fundamental protocol for serial data transmission in embedded systems. We explored how to configure and use UART to send and receive data between a microcontroller and a computer. This communication is essential for interfacing microcontrollers with other systems, such as sensors, displays, or computers. UART's simplicity, efficiency, and widespread use make it a core protocol in embedded systems development.

Chapter 9: Communication Protocols: SPI and I2C

SPI and I2C Basics

In embedded systems, communication protocols are crucial for enabling the interaction between a microcontroller and peripheral devices. Among the most widely used protocols are **SPI (Serial Peripheral Interface)** and **I2C (Inter-Integrated Circuit)**. Both protocols are used for connecting multiple devices to a microcontroller, but they each have different characteristics, use cases, and advantages. Understanding the differences between these protocols is important for selecting the right one for your application.

- **What is SPI (Serial Peripheral Interface)?** SPI is a synchronous serial communication protocol used for high-speed data exchange between a microcontroller and one or more peripheral devices (e.g., sensors, memory chips, displays). It works by using a master-slave configuration, where the microcontroller acts as the **master** and communicates with peripheral **slaves**.
  - **Key Features of SPI:**
    - Full-duplex communication: Data can be sent and received simultaneously.

- High-speed communication: Typically faster than I2C due to its simpler protocol.
- Dedicated lines for communication:
  - **MOSI (Master Out Slave In)**
  - **MISO (Master In Slave Out)**
  - **SCK (Clock)**
  - **SS (Slave Select)**
  - o **Use Case:** SPI is well-suited for applications that require fast data transfer over short distances, such as **SD card communication**, **LCD screens**, or **ADC/DAC** conversions.
- **What is I2C (Inter-Integrated Circuit)?** I2C is another synchronous serial communication protocol but uses fewer wires than SPI. It is a two-wire communication protocol (SDA and SCL) and can support multiple devices (both master and slave) on the same bus.
  - o **Key Features of I2C:**
    - Half-duplex communication: Data is either sent or received, not simultaneously.
    - Uses only two lines: **SDA (Serial Data)** and **SCL (Serial Clock)**.
    - Each device on the bus has a unique address, which allows multiple devices to share the same bus.

- Slower than SPI but more flexible due to the ability to address multiple devices.
  - **Use Case:** I2C is ideal for **sensor networks**, **EEPROMs**, and **RTC modules** where the communication speed is not critical, and reducing the number of wires is more important.

Programming SPI and I2C in C

Both SPI and I2C require initialization, setting up of the communication speed (baud rate), and configuring the relevant pins to communicate with external devices. We'll explore how to implement both protocols in C, using specific microcontroller registers and functions.

- **Programming SPI in C:**

  To begin SPI communication, the following steps are typically involved:

  1. **Set Up the SPI Pins:**
     - MOSI, MISO, SCK, and SS must be configured as output/input pins depending on whether the device is the master or slave.
  2. **Configure the SPI Settings:**
     - Set the baud rate (communication speed).
     - Configure the clock polarity and phase (CPOL and CPHA).

3. **Send and Receive Data:**
   - Use the SPI data register to transmit and receive data.

Example: SPI Initialization for STM32

c

```c
void SPI_Init(void) {
    // Configure SPI peripheral settings
    SPI1->CR1 |= SPI_CR1_MSTR;  // Set SPI as master
    SPI1->CR1 |= SPI_CR1_BR;    // Set baud rate
    SPI1->CR1 |= SPI_CR1_SPE;   // Enable SPI
}

uint8_t SPI_Transmit(uint8_t data) {
    while (!(SPI1->SR & SPI_SR_TXE));  // Wait for TX buffer to be empty
    SPI1->DR = data;            // Write data to the SPI data register
    while (!(SPI1->SR & SPI_SR_RXNE));  // Wait for RX buffer to be not empty
    return SPI1->DR;            // Read received data
}
```

- **Programming I2C in C:**

I2C communication is typically initiated by sending the address of the device followed by the data. The key components include the data register and the clock line.

1. **Set Up I2C Pins:**

   - SDA and SCL must be configured for I2C functionality.

2. **Configure the I2C Speed and Address:**

   - Define the clock speed for I2C and the 7-bit address of the device to communicate with.

3. **Send and Receive Data:**

   - Initiate communication by sending the start condition, followed by the device address and data.

Example: I2C Initialization for STM32

c

```c
void I2C_Init(void) {
    // Configure I2C settings for master mode
    I2C1->CR1 |= I2C_CR1_PE; // Enable I2C peripheral
    I2C1->CCR = 0x28;       // Set I2C clock control register for desired frequency
}

void I2C_Transmit(uint8_t address, uint8_t data) {
    I2C1->DR = address;    // Write address to the data register
    while (!(I2C1->SR1 & I2C_SR1_SB)); // Wait for start bit
    I2C1->DR = data;       // Write data to be transmitted
    while (!(I2C1->SR1 & I2C_SR1_BTF)); // Wait for byte transfer to finish
}
```

Real-World Example: Communicating with an LCD Display Using SPI or I2C

In this example, we will interface a microcontroller with an **LCD display**. LCD displays often use SPI or I2C communication to interact with a microcontroller. This allows you to easily display text or other information on the screen.

- **Using SPI for LCD Communication:** When using SPI to communicate with an LCD, you would typically send command bytes and data bytes in a sequence. Here's how it might look in C:

c

```c
// Function to initialize LCD using SPI
void LCD_Init(void) {
    SPI_Init();  // Initialize SPI
    SPI_Transmit(0x38);  // Send initialization command
    SPI_Transmit(0x0C);  // Display ON, cursor OFF
}

// Function to send data to LCD
void LCD_SendData(uint8_t data) {
    SPI_Transmit(data);  // Send data byte to LCD
}
```

- **Using I2C for LCD Communication:** For I2C, communication would involve sending the LCD's address along with command and data bytes:

c

```
// Function to initialize LCD using I2C
void LCD_Init(void) {
    I2C_Init();  // Initialize I2C
    I2C_Transmit(0x27, 0x38);  // Send initialization command (address: 0x27)
    I2C_Transmit(0x27, 0x0C);  // Display ON, cursor OFF
}

// Function to send data to LCD
void LCD_SendData(uint8_t data) {
    I2C_Transmit(0x27, data);  // Send data byte to LCD
}
```

In both cases, the communication between the microcontroller and the LCD is done by sending specific commands and data. Depending on your system's design, you can choose between SPI and I2C based on the number of devices you need to connect and the desired speed of communication.

Key Takeaways:

- **SPI and I2C** are both widely used communication protocols in embedded systems, each with its strengths and use cases.
- **SPI** is fast and ideal for short-distance, high-speed data transfer with a limited number of devices.
- **I2C** is more flexible for connecting multiple devices with fewer pins, although it is slower than SPI.
- Interfacing with peripherals like an LCD using either SPI or I2C allows for building more complex embedded systems with minimal wiring.

Chapter 10: Working with Sensors and Actuators

In the world of embedded systems, sensors and actuators are key components for making real-world interactions possible. **Sensors** allow microcontrollers to collect data from the environment, while **actuators** enable microcontrollers to interact with and control external systems. This chapter will cover the basics of interfacing with both types of devices and provide practical examples that will be useful for building real-world applications.

Interfacing with Sensors

Sensors convert physical quantities (like temperature, pressure, light intensity, etc.) into electrical signals that microcontrollers can read and process. Depending on the type of sensor, the microcontroller can receive data in either **analog** or **digital** form.

Common Types of Sensors:

- **Temperature Sensors**: These sensors measure the ambient temperature and convert it into an electrical signal. Common types include thermistors, thermocouples, and digital temperature sensors like the **DHT11** or **DS18B20**.

- **Humidity Sensors**: These sensors measure the humidity level in the air. Sensors like the **DHT22** are often used for weather stations.

- **Distance Sensors**: These sensors measure the distance to an object, commonly used in applications like robotics for obstacle detection. Examples include **Ultrasonic sensors (HC-SR04)** and **Infrared (IR) sensors**.

- **Light Sensors**: These sensors detect the intensity of light and are often used in applications like automatic lighting control. A **photoresistor (LDR)** is a common light sensor.

Analog vs Digital Sensors:

- **Analog Sensors**: These sensors output a continuous voltage that corresponds to the physical parameter being measured (e.g., temperature, light intensity). To interface with these sensors, you typically need to use the **Analog-to-Digital Converter (ADC)** on the microcontroller to convert the analog signal to a digital value.

- **Digital Sensors**: These sensors output a discrete signal (usually HIGH or LOW) or a serial signal that can be read directly by the microcontroller. Examples include digital temperature sensors like **DHT11** or **DS18B20**.

Interfacing with a Temperature Sensor (e.g., DHT11)

1. **Connecting the Sensor**: The **DHT11** is a popular digital temperature and humidity sensor. It has three pins: VCC (power), GND (ground), and **Data** (used for communication). To interface it with a microcontroller like Arduino or STM32, connect the **Data** pin to a GPIO pin on the microcontroller, with a pull-up resistor (usually 10kΩ) connected between the **Data** pin and **VCC**.

2. **Reading Data**: To read data from the sensor, you can use a dedicated library (e.g., DHT.h for Arduino) or write your own code to handle the timing and communication protocol. The DHT11 sensor sends temperature and humidity data in a pre-defined 40-bit format (8 bits for humidity, 8 bits for temperature, and a checksum).

Example Code for Reading a Temperature Sensor:

c

```c
#include <DHT.h>   // Include the DHT sensor library

#define DHTPIN 2   // Pin where the sensor is connected
#define DHTTYPE DHT11   // Define the sensor type

DHT dht(DHTPIN, DHTTYPE);  // Initialize the sensor

void setup() {
  Serial.begin(9600); // Initialize serial communication
  dht.begin();  // Initialize the DHT sensor
}
```

```
void loop() {
  float humidity = dht.readHumidity();  // Read humidity
  float temperature = dht.readTemperature();  // Read temperature

  if (isnan(humidity) || isnan(temperature)) {
    Serial.println("Failed to read from DHT sensor!");
    return;
  }

  Serial.print("Temperature: ");
  Serial.print(temperature);
  Serial.print(" °C  Humidity: ");
  Serial.print(humidity);
  Serial.println(" %");
  delay(2000);  // Wait for 2 seconds before next reading
}
```

Interfacing with Actuators

Actuators are devices that take action based on the control signals they receive from the microcontroller. These can include motors, relays, solenoids, and more. In embedded systems, actuators are used to drive mechanical movement, control external devices, or perform any action that requires physical intervention.

Types of Actuators:

- **Motors**: Motors are commonly used to drive mechanical movement. **DC motors**, **servo motors**, and **stepper motors** are examples of motors frequently used in embedded systems.

- **Relays**: Relays are used to control high-power devices (like lights or appliances) through low-power control signals from the microcontroller.

- **Solenoids**: These are used to generate linear motion when an electrical current is passed through them, commonly used in locking mechanisms or automated systems.

- **LEDs**: Though simple, LEDs are common actuators used for indicating system status or user feedback.

Example: Controlling a DC Motor with PWM

Pulse Width Modulation (**PWM**) is a technique used to control the speed of DC motors by varying the duty cycle of a square wave signal. A higher duty cycle means the motor runs faster, and a lower duty cycle results in a slower speed.

1. **Connecting the Motor**: A DC motor can be connected to a microcontroller through a motor driver (e.g., L298N). The motor driver acts as an interface between the microcontroller's GPIO pins and the motor, protecting the microcontroller from high currents.

2. **Controlling the Motor**: You can control the speed of the DC motor by adjusting the PWM signal sent to the motor driver.

Example Code for Motor Control with PWM:

c

```
#define motorPin 9   // Pin connected to the motor driver

void setup() {
  pinMode(motorPin, OUTPUT);  // Set the motor control pin as an output
}

void loop() {
  // Motor runs at full speed
  analogWrite(motorPin, 255);   // 255 is the maximum PWM value (100% duty cycle)
  delay(2000);  // Run the motor for 2 seconds

  // Motor slows down gradually
  for (int i = 255; i >= 0; i--) {
    analogWrite(motorPin, i);   // Decrease PWM value
    delay(20);  // Wait 20ms before updating the PWM value
  }

  delay(2000);  // Pause before the next iteration
}
```

Real-World Example: Building a Simple Weather Station

By combining sensors and actuators, you can build practical applications that gather and present real-world data. A **simple weather station** is a perfect example of how sensors and actuators work together. In this case, we will interface with a **DHT11 temperature and humidity sensor** to collect environmental data, display the readings on an **LCD** or **OLED display**, and even use an **LED** to indicate if the temperature exceeds a certain threshold.

Steps to Build a Weather Station:

1. **Connect the DHT11 sensor** to the microcontroller (e.g., Arduino or STM32).
2. **Set up an LCD or OLED display** to show the temperature and humidity readings.
3. **Add a temperature threshold**: If the temperature exceeds a certain value, turn on an LED to indicate a high temperature alert.
4. **Add functionality for periodic readings**: Program the microcontroller to take measurements every few seconds and display the updated readings on the display.

Full Example Code for Weather Station:

c

```
#include <DHT.h>
#include <Wire.h>
#include <LiquidCrystal_I2C.h>
```

```c
#define DHTPIN 2
#define DHTTYPE DHT11

DHT dht(DHTPIN, DHTTYPE);
LiquidCrystal_I2C lcd(0x27, 16, 2);  // Set the LCD address and size

int ledPin = 13;  // Pin connected to the LED

void setup() {
  lcd.begin(16, 2);
  lcd.print("Weather Station");
  dht.begin();
  pinMode(ledPin, OUTPUT);  // Set LED pin as an output
  delay(2000);  // Wait for the sensor to stabilize
}

void loop() {
  float humidity = dht.readHumidity();
  float temperature = dht.readTemperature();

  if (isnan(humidity) || isnan(temperature)) {
   lcd.clear();
   lcd.print("Sensor error");
   return;
  }

  lcd.clear();
  lcd.print("Temp: ");
  lcd.print(temperature);
```

```
lcd.print(" C");

lcd.setCursor(0, 1);
lcd.print("Humidity: ");
lcd.print(humidity);
lcd.print(" %");

if (temperature > 30) {
  digitalWrite(ledPin, HIGH);  // Turn on LED if temp > 30
} else {
  digitalWrite(ledPin, LOW);  // Turn off LED if temp <= 30
}

delay(2000);  // Wait 2 seconds before the next reading
}
```

:

Working with sensors and actuators is a fundamental part of embedded systems programming. By interfacing with various sensors, you can collect data from the environment, and by using actuators, you can take action based on that data. This chapter provided insights into working with common sensors (e.g., temperature, humidity) and actuators (e.g., motors, LEDs) and demonstrated how to build practical projects like weather stations and simple control systems. By mastering these techniques, you will

Chapter 11: PWM – Pulse Width Modulation

Pulse Width Modulation (PWM) is one of the most powerful techniques used in embedded systems for controlling the power delivered to electronic components. From adjusting the brightness of LEDs to controlling the speed of motors, PWM allows precise control using a simple digital signal. This chapter explores how PWM works, how to program it in C, and how it can be applied in real-world engineering projects.

What is PWM?

PWM is a method of controlling the amount of power delivered to a device by varying the width of the pulses in a square wave signal. Instead of adjusting the voltage directly, PWM works by rapidly switching the signal between ON and OFF states. The ratio of time the signal stays ON (high) compared to when it is OFF (low) is called the **duty cycle**.

- **Duty Cycle**: The percentage of time the signal stays ON during each cycle. For example, a 50% duty cycle means the signal is ON for half of the time and OFF for the other half.

- **Frequency**: The rate at which the PWM signal oscillates, typically measured in Hertz (Hz). It determines how fast the ON/OFF cycles occur.

PWM Example:

- If you want to control an LED's brightness, a 100% duty cycle means the LED is fully ON (always receiving power), while a 0% duty cycle means the LED is completely OFF. A 50% duty cycle would mean the LED is on half the time, appearing dimmer than when it's fully ON.

PWM can be used to simulate analog control by rapidly switching between full ON and OFF states at a high frequency, so the human eye or motor responds as if it's receiving a continuous analog signal.

Programming PWM in C

Microcontrollers have dedicated hardware peripherals, such as timers, that can generate PWM signals automatically without requiring a lot of software processing. However, understanding how to configure these peripherals using C is essential for creating custom applications.

Steps for Setting Up PWM in C:

1. **Configure the Timer**: Microcontrollers typically have timers or counter modules that can be configured to generate PWM signals. You can set the timer's period (frequency) and duty cycle.

2. **Configure PWM Pin**: You'll need to assign a microcontroller pin as an output for PWM. Often, this is done through the **GPIO** (General Purpose Input/Output) pin configuration.

3. **Calculate Duty Cycle**: For example, to achieve a 50% duty cycle, set the compare value of the timer to half the timer's period.

4. **Start the PWM Signal**: Once everything is configured, the microcontroller will automatically start generating the PWM signal.

Example of a Simple PWM Setup in C:

c

```
// Example code for setting up PWM using Timer in STM32
void PWM_Init() {
    // Configure GPIO pin as PWM output
    GPIO_Init(GPIOB,          GPIO_Pin_0,          GPIO_Mode_AF_PP,
GPIO_Speed_50MHz);

    // Enable the PWM timer (e.g., Timer 2)
    TIM_TimeBaseInitTypeDef timerConfig;
    timerConfig.TIM_Prescaler = 72 - 1; // Set timer prescaler
    timerConfig.TIM_Period = 1000 - 1;  // Set the PWM period (frequency)
```

```
    timerConfig.TIM_ClockDivision = TIM_CKD_DIV1;
    timerConfig.TIM_CounterMode = TIM_CounterMode_Up;
    TIM_TimeBaseInit(TIM2, &timerConfig);

    // Set PWM duty cycle (e.g., 50% duty cycle)
    TIM_OCInitTypeDef pwmConfig;
    pwmConfig.TIM_OCMode = TIM_OCMode_PWM1;
    pwmConfig.TIM_OutputState = TIM_OutputState_Enable;
    pwmConfig.TIM_OCPolarity = TIM_OCPolarity_High;
    pwmConfig.TIM_Pulse = 500; // Duty cycle (50%)
    TIM_OC1Init(TIM2, &pwmConfig);

    // Enable the timer and start PWM output
    TIM_Cmd(TIM2, ENABLE);
    TIM_OC1PreloadConfig(TIM2, TIM_OCPreload_Enable);
}
```

Real-World Example: Controlling the Brightness of an LED and Speed of a DC Motor

PWM is commonly used in embedded systems to control the brightness of LEDs and the speed of DC motors. These applications require the microcontroller to adjust the duty cycle of the PWM signal to vary the power delivered to the devices.

Controlling LED Brightness with PWM:

An LED's brightness is controlled by adjusting the duty cycle of the PWM signal. By increasing the duty cycle, you increase the amount of time the LED is ON, making it appear brighter. Conversely, by reducing the duty cycle, the LED appears dimmer.

Example:

- **50% Duty Cycle**: The LED is on half the time, so it appears at half brightness.
- **100% Duty Cycle**: The LED is fully on and at maximum brightness.

Controlling Motor Speed with PWM:

PWM is also commonly used to control the speed of DC motors. By adjusting the duty cycle, the effective voltage supplied to the motor is varied, thus controlling its speed.

Example:

- **100% Duty Cycle**: The motor runs at full speed because the motor is receiving a constant voltage.
- **50% Duty Cycle**: The motor runs at half speed because it is being powered for only half of each cycle.

Example of Motor Speed Control Code:

c

```c
// Example code for controlling motor speed using PWM
void Motor_PWM_Init() {
    // Configure PWM as done previously
    PWM_Init(); // Initialize PWM signal
```

```
// Set the desired motor speed using PWM duty cycle (e.g., 75% speed)
TIM_OC1Init(TIM2, 750); // Set PWM pulse width to 75% duty cycle

// Start the motor with PWM control
TIM_Cmd(TIM2, ENABLE);
}
```

This function would control the speed of the motor by adjusting the duty cycle of the PWM signal sent to the motor driver circuit.

PWM is a critical tool for controlling devices like LEDs, motors, and other actuators in embedded systems. In this chapter, you learned the basics of PWM, how to configure PWM signals using C, and real-world applications of PWM in controlling the brightness of LEDs and the speed of DC motors. By mastering PWM, you can build more efficient and responsive embedded systems capable of interacting with the real world in a variety of ways.

Chapter 12: Power Management in Embedded Systems

Power management is a crucial aspect of designing embedded systems, especially for battery-powered devices and applications that need to run for extended periods without frequent recharging. Efficient power usage not only extends battery life but also ensures that the system operates reliably and efficiently. This chapter focuses on techniques for reducing power consumption, the role of sleep modes, and practical strategies for building low-power systems.

Power Consumption in Embedded Systems

One of the primary considerations in embedded system design is power consumption, particularly when the system is intended to run on battery power. Whether you're building a portable device, a sensor network, or a remote monitoring system, managing power is essential for maintaining functionality over time. Power consumption is determined by the active operation of components such as the microcontroller, sensors, actuators, and communication modules.

Factors Affecting Power Consumption:

- **Microcontroller Power Draw:** Different microcontrollers have varying levels of power consumption depending on their clock speed, processing load, and operating voltage. Lower-power microcontrollers (e.g., ARM Cortex-M, AVR) are specifically designed for battery-operated applications.

- **Peripheral Power Usage:** Sensors, displays, and communication modules (e.g., Bluetooth, Wi-Fi) consume different amounts of power based on their activity. Active sensors may draw a lot of power, while idle components use minimal power.

- **Communication Protocols:** Wireless communication (e.g., Wi-Fi, Bluetooth) can be a major source of power consumption. Managing the frequency of communication and reducing data transmission can help conserve energy.

Techniques for Reducing Power Consumption:

- **Clock Management:** Reducing the clock speed of the microcontroller can significantly decrease power usage. Many microcontrollers offer dynamic frequency scaling, allowing them to adjust their clock speed based on the workload.

- **Power Gating:** Disabling unused peripherals or modules can reduce power consumption. For example, turning off the ADC, UART, or communication interfaces when they are not in use.

- **Dynamic Power Management:** Implementing algorithms that adjust the power usage of different system components based on the workload. This ensures that the system uses the minimum amount of power necessary for the task at hand.

Sleep Modes and Low-Power Operation

One of the most effective ways to manage power consumption is by utilizing **sleep modes** and **low-power operation** techniques. These modes are designed to reduce power consumption when the system is idle or performing minimal tasks, and they can be used to extend the operational time of battery-powered devices.

Types of Sleep Modes:

- **Idle Mode:** The CPU is paused, but peripherals such as timers, clocks, and communication modules may still be active. The system consumes low power but can quickly resume operation.
- **Sleep Mode:** The CPU and most peripherals are powered down, but specific peripherals (e.g., watchdog timers or external interrupts) remain active to wake up the system.
- **Deep Sleep Mode:** The microcontroller enters a state where almost all functions are halted, except for essential tasks like maintaining the real-time clock. This is the

lowest power consumption mode and is suitable for long periods of inactivity.

- **Standby Mode:** A more extreme power-saving mode where even fewer components are running, minimizing energy usage to the absolute minimum.

Wake-Up Sources:

- **Timers:** A timer can trigger the system to wake up after a specific time interval, useful for tasks that need periodic measurements or actions.
- **External Interrupts:** External events such as a button press, motion detection, or sensor threshold crossing can be used to wake up the system from sleep mode.
- **Communication Events:** Communication modules like UART, I2C, or SPI can be set up to wake the system up upon receiving data or signals.

Incorporating these low-power modes is essential for building efficient embedded systems, especially those that require long battery life.

Real-World Example: Building a Battery-Powered Sensor Node That Operates on Low Power

To illustrate the concepts of power management, let's consider a real-world example: building a **battery-powered environmental sensor node**. This node could be used in applications like remote weather stations, health monitoring systems, or smart agriculture.

System Requirements:

- A **temperature and humidity sensor** to monitor environmental conditions.
- A microcontroller (e.g., an ARM Cortex-M based MCU) to process sensor data.
- A wireless module (e.g., LoRa, Bluetooth) to transmit data to a central system.
- A battery-powered system that needs to last for months or even years.

Step 1: Selecting the Components

- **Microcontroller**: Choose an energy-efficient microcontroller that supports low-power modes. For example, the STM32L series or the ESP32 have excellent low-power capabilities.
- **Sensor**: Select a low-power sensor, such as the DHT11 or BME280, that operates at low voltage and consumes minimal current during measurements.

- **Wireless Communication**: Use a low-power communication module, like LoRa, which can operate in low-power modes and supports long-range transmission.

Step 2: Low-Power Design

- **Sleep Mode**: The microcontroller will remain in sleep mode most of the time, waking up periodically (e.g., every 10 minutes) to take a sensor reading and transmit data.
- **Power Gating**: The wireless communication module and sensor will be powered down when not in use, drawing no current until it's time to take a measurement.
- **Timer Interrupts**: Use a timer interrupt to wake up the microcontroller every 10 minutes to perform a reading.
- **Data Transmission**: Only transmit data during specific intervals, minimizing the time the wireless module is active.

Step 3: Optimizing Battery Life

- **Duty Cycle**: Set the system's duty cycle to maximize battery life. For instance, the sensor could take a reading for 1 second, transmit the data for 3 seconds, and then remain in low-power mode for 9 minutes.
- **Battery Selection**: Choose a battery with a suitable capacity, such as a Li-ion or Li-Po battery, to ensure it can power the sensor node for a long period.

Step 4: Testing and Evaluation

- **Measure Current Consumption**: Use a multimeter to measure the current draw in different states (active, sleep, and deep sleep) to ensure the system's total consumption is within the desired limits.

- **Battery Life Calculation**: Calculate the expected battery life based on the current consumption and the capacity of the chosen battery.

By following these steps, you can create a battery-powered sensor node that runs for an extended period while maintaining efficient power usage. This low-power design approach can be applied to many other battery-operated embedded systems, ensuring that your devices can run autonomously for long periods, even in remote or inaccessible locations.

This chapter highlighted key strategies for power management in embedded systems, including the use of sleep modes, power gating, and efficient design choices to minimize energy consumption. In the next chapter, we will delve into advanced techniques for optimizing performance while maintaining low power consumption in more complex systems.

Chapter 13: Debugging and Testing Embedded Systems

Debugging and testing embedded systems can be challenging due to their real-time, hardware-dependent nature. Unlike traditional software development, embedded systems interact directly with physical components, which can introduce unique issues such as hardware malfunctions, timing problems, and low-level communication failures. This chapter covers tools and techniques for effectively debugging embedded systems, common issues engineers face, and real-world examples of troubleshooting typical embedded system problems.

Tools for Debugging

Effective debugging in embedded systems requires a combination of software tools and hardware techniques. While traditional debugging methods (like print statements and log files) work in standard software development, embedded systems demand more specialized approaches due to their tight coupling with hardware.

1. Serial Output for Debugging:

- **Overview:** Serial communication (often through UART) is one of the most common methods for debugging embedded systems. By sending data over a serial interface to a computer, engineers can view system states, variable values, and error messages in real-time.

- **Implementation:** Utilize printf() or other logging functions in your code to send debugging information to a serial terminal.
- **Use Cases:** Monitor sensor values, track system status, or inspect intermediate variables for troubleshooting.

2. LEDs for Debugging:

- **Overview:** LEDs are often used for simple status indicators in embedded systems. They are useful for debugging when serial communication is unavailable, or you need quick feedback on system behavior.
- **Implementation:** Use different LED patterns (blinking, on/off) to indicate various system states such as power-up, error conditions, or communication status.
- **Use Cases:** Blink an LED when a button is pressed, or use two LEDs to show the progress of a communication attempt.

3. External Debuggers (JTAG, SWD, etc.):

- **Overview:** External debugging tools such as JTAG (Joint Test Action Group) and SWD (Serial Wire Debug) provide powerful debugging capabilities. These tools allow you to halt the microcontroller, inspect memory, step through code, and even modify variables during runtime.

- **Implementation:** Connect a debugger to the microcontroller's debug interface, set breakpoints, and trace execution.
- **Use Cases:** Use the debugger to examine the call stack, register values, and inspect memory, making it easier to identify bugs in both hardware and software.

4. In-Circuit Emulators (ICE):

- **Overview:** ICE is a hardware debugging tool that can emulate the microcontroller's behavior. It allows you to run and test embedded software on real hardware with full visibility and control.
- **Implementation:** Connect an ICE to the target hardware, then use the development environment to load and execute the software in real time.
- **Use Cases:** Helps with debugging complex timing and real-time systems issues, especially those related to low-level hardware interactions.

Common Issues in Embedded Systems

Embedded systems involve complex interactions between hardware and software, which makes them prone to specific types of issues. Below are some of the most common problems encountered when debugging embedded systems:

1. Communication Issues (UART, SPI, I2C, etc.):

- **Problem:** Communication between components or with external devices can fail due to incorrect baud rates, mismatched protocols, faulty wiring, or software bugs.
- **Solution:** Use serial output to check the transmission and reception of data. Oscilloscopes or logic analyzers can help inspect the signal integrity and timing of communication lines.

2. Memory Corruption and Buffer Overflows:

- **Problem:** Buffer overflows, stack overflows, or memory corruption can occur when data is written beyond the allocated memory. This could cause crashes, unpredictable behavior, or data loss.
- **Solution:** Use debugging tools to inspect memory, enable stack protection in the compiler, and check for off-by-one errors in buffer management. External debuggers and logging can also help in tracking down where the overflow occurs.

3. Timing and Synchronization Problems:

- **Problem:** Embedded systems often operate in real-time, which means that precise timing is crucial. Issues such as task scheduling, interrupt handling, and timing mismatches can cause systems to fail.

- **Solution:** Use timers and interrupts to ensure that tasks are executed at the correct time. Tools like oscilloscopes and logic analyzers are valuable for checking timing precision and synchronizing different components.

4. Power-Related Issues:

- **Problem:** Unstable power supplies, voltage drops, or power spikes can lead to malfunctioning hardware or corrupted software.

- **Solution:** Use a multimeter or oscilloscope to monitor power levels and verify that power is within the acceptable range. Employ low-power modes and ensure that power sequences are correctly handled.

Real-World Example: Debugging a UART Communication Problem

One of the most common issues in embedded systems is improper UART communication. This could manifest as failure to send or receive data correctly, garbled characters, or even no communication at all.

Scenario: You are working on a project where a microcontroller sends data to a PC over UART. However, the data received on the PC is corrupted, and you're unable to interpret it correctly.

Step 1: Verify the Baud Rate and Parameters

- **Problem:** Mismatch between the baud rate of the microcontroller and the PC can lead to corrupted data.
- **Solution:** Double-check the baud rate, parity bit, data bit, and stop bit settings in both the microcontroller code and the terminal program on the PC. Make sure they are the same.

Step 2: Use Serial Output for Debugging

- **Problem:** You cannot confirm whether the microcontroller is transmitting the correct data.
- **Solution:** Insert debug prints into your code to send status updates to the serial monitor. If the microcontroller is correctly generating the data, you should see this in the serial output.

Step 3: Use LEDs for Quick Feedback

- **Problem:** The microcontroller might be stuck in an error state or not reaching the UART transmission code.

- **Solution:** Set up an LED to blink at regular intervals in the program. If the LED doesn't blink as expected, you know the microcontroller is not entering the correct state.

Step 4: Use an Oscilloscope or Logic Analyzer

- **Problem:** Even after checking the settings, the data might still be corrupted, possibly due to physical issues like noise on the communication lines.
- **Solution:** Use a logic analyzer or oscilloscope to monitor the data being transmitted over the TX line of the microcontroller. Check for voltage level mismatches or timing issues that may be causing bit errors.

Step 5: Cross-Check the Data on Both Sides

- **Problem:** You suspect a fault in the receiving code on the PC.
- **Solution:** Monitor the received data on both the microcontroller side and the PC side. Use a known good UART communication example to test the receiving side of the PC code. Ensure that the serial buffer is being handled correctly and that there is no overflow or data loss.

By following these steps, you can systematically troubleshoot a UART communication problem and apply the same principles to other forms of communication or embedded system issues. The key to successful debugging in embedded systems is persistence, using the right tools, and thinking through the system's operation from both the software and hardware perspectives.

Chapter 14: Memory Management in Embedded Systems

Memory management is a critical aspect of embedded system design. Unlike general-purpose computing systems, embedded systems often have constrained resources, including limited memory and processing power. Efficient memory usage is key to optimizing performance and ensuring that the system operates reliably over long periods, especially in resource-constrained environments like battery-powered applications.

This chapter will explore memory types commonly used in embedded systems, discuss memory management techniques, and provide real-world examples to highlight how embedded system developers can efficiently manage memory.

Memory Considerations for Embedded Systems
1. Types of Memory in Embedded Systems:

Embedded systems typically use different types of memory to store both executable code and data. The three most common types are **RAM**, **Flash**, and **EEPROM**.

- ### RAM (Random Access Memory):

- **Characteristics:** RAM is a volatile memory that stores data temporarily while the system is running. It is used for variables, program stack, and dynamically allocated memory.

- **Use in Embedded Systems:** RAM in embedded systems is often limited in size, and its management is crucial for maintaining system stability and performance. Efficient use of RAM can help prevent memory overflow or corruption, which is common in systems with limited resources.

- **Flash Memory:**

  - **Characteristics:** Flash memory is a non-volatile storage medium used to store the firmware or executable code for embedded systems. Data in flash memory is retained even when the system is powered off.

  - **Use in Embedded Systems:** Flash memory is used for storing the main program code and configuration settings. It is typically slower than RAM but is necessary for long-term storage. Flash is usually divided into sections for code (program memory) and data (data storage).

- **EEPROM (Electrically Erasable Programmable Read-Only Memory):**

- o **Characteristics:** EEPROM is a type of non-volatile memory that allows for small amounts of data to be written and read multiple times.

- o **Use in Embedded Systems:** EEPROM is commonly used to store configuration settings, calibration data, or logs that need to persist between reboots. Its write endurance is lower than that of flash, but it's useful for storing small amounts of critical data that must be preserved.

2. Memory Management in Embedded Systems:

Efficient memory management is essential for the proper functioning of embedded systems. Given the limited memory available, it is important to optimize both the use of RAM and non-volatile memory.

- **Stack vs. Heap Memory Management:**
  - o **Stack Memory:** The stack is used for storing local variables, function arguments, and return addresses. It grows and shrinks dynamically as functions are called and return, respectively. Care must be taken to prevent stack overflows, which can crash the system.
  - o **Heap Memory:** The heap is used for dynamically allocated memory during runtime. It requires

careful management to prevent memory fragmentation and leaks. In embedded systems with limited RAM, it's important to minimize dynamic memory allocation.

- **Static vs. Dynamic Memory Allocation:**
  - ○ **Static Allocation:** In this method, memory is allocated at compile time, and the size of variables is fixed. This approach is typically more efficient and less error-prone, but it lacks flexibility.
  - ○ **Dynamic Allocation:** Memory is allocated at runtime. This can be more flexible but requires more care in managing memory blocks to avoid fragmentation and leaks.

- **Memory Fragmentation:**
  - ○ Fragmentation occurs when memory is allocated and freed over time, causing free memory to be split into smaller, non-contiguous blocks. This can lead to inefficient use of memory, especially in systems with limited RAM.

- **Memory Pools:**
  - ○ Memory pools are pre-allocated blocks of memory used for fixed-size objects, which help minimize fragmentation. A memory pool system allows for more predictable and efficient memory usage,

especially in embedded applications that require high reliability.

Real-World Example: Storing Configuration Data in EEPROM

In embedded systems, configuration data (e.g., user settings, calibration data) often needs to be stored persistently across reboots. EEPROM is ideal for this purpose because of its non-volatile nature.

In this example, we'll build a simple program that stores configuration data in EEPROM using an AVR microcontroller (e.g., ATmega328P), which has built-in EEPROM support.

Objective:

- Write a program that stores and retrieves a configuration value (e.g., system threshold) in EEPROM.

Step-by-Step Example:

1. **Define the EEPROM Address:**
   o EEPROM has a limited number of write cycles, so it is important to write only when necessary. We'll store a threshold value at a specific memory address.

c

#define EEPROM_THRESHOLD_ADDRESS 0x00 // Address for threshold value in EEPROM

2. Write Function to EEPROM:

o   Use the built-in EEPROM.write() function to store data. This function writes a byte to the specified address.

c

```
#include <avr/io.h>
#include <avr/eeprom.h>

void storeThreshold(uint8_t threshold) {
  eeprom_write_byte((uint8_t*)EEPROM_THRESHOLD_ADDRESS, threshold);  // Store value at the specified address
}
```

3. Read Function from EEPROM:

o   Use the EEPROM.read() function to retrieve the stored value.

c

```
uint8_t readThreshold() {
  return   eeprom_read_byte((uint8_t*)EEPROM_THRESHOLD_ADDRESS);
// Retrieve value from the specified address
}
```

4. Main Program Logic:

     o   In the main program, we can store a new threshold value and then read it back for use.

c

```
int main() {
    uint8_t threshold = 50;  // Set a default threshold value
    storeThreshold(threshold);  // Store the threshold in EEPROM

    // Simulate reading the stored threshold after a reset
    uint8_t storedThreshold = readThreshold();

    // Use the stored threshold for system control (e.g., trigger an action based on
the threshold)

    while (1) {
        // Main program loop
    }
}
```

5. **Optimizing EEPROM Usage:**

     o   Since EEPROM has a limited number of write cycles, it's important to avoid unnecessary writes. For example, only write to EEPROM if the configuration value has changed.

c

```
if (newThreshold != storedThreshold) {
```

storeThreshold(newThreshold); // Only store if the threshold has changed
}

Explanation:

- In this example, the configuration data (a threshold value) is stored in EEPROM and can be read back after a system reboot. By using EEPROM's non-volatile storage capability, we ensure that the configuration persists even when the system is powered off.
- The example also demonstrates a simple method to avoid unnecessary writes, which helps to extend the lifespan of the EEPROM.

Memory management is a key aspect of embedded systems programming. Understanding the different types of memory (RAM, Flash, EEPROM) and how to efficiently manage them is essential for creating reliable and high-performance embedded systems. In this chapter, we explored various memory management techniques and provided practical examples of using EEPROM to store persistent data in embedded systems. As embedded systems become more sophisticated, careful memory management will continue to be critical for optimizing performance, reducing power consumption, and increasing system reliability.

Chapter 15: Building Embedded Systems for IoT

The **Internet of Things (IoT)** is a rapidly growing field where everyday objects are connected to the internet, allowing them to send and receive data. This chapter will guide you through the basics of using **microcontrollers** to build IoT devices, covering the hardware, communication protocols, and software involved in creating connected systems.

Embedded systems form the backbone of IoT, where **microcontrollers** (MCUs) are often used to collect data, control devices, and communicate with other systems over the internet. In this chapter, we'll explore how microcontrollers can be leveraged for IoT applications, including communication protocols like **Wi-Fi**, **Bluetooth**, and **LoRa**.

---

1. Introduction to IoT and Microcontrollers
What is IoT?

- The **Internet of Things (IoT)** refers to the network of devices connected to the internet that can collect and exchange data with minimal human intervention. These devices range from smart home products (thermostats, lights, security cameras) to industrial sensors and health monitoring equipment.

- In the IoT ecosystem, **microcontrollers** serve as the "brains" of these devices. They collect data from sensors, process it, and communicate with other devices or the cloud via wireless communication protocols.

Microcontrollers in IoT:

- Microcontrollers are essential in IoT devices because they are small, power-efficient, and capable of running embedded software to interface with sensors, actuators, and communication modules.
- Popular microcontrollers for IoT applications include:
  - **ESP32**: A popular microcontroller with built-in **Wi-Fi** and **Bluetooth** capabilities.
  - **ESP8266**: A less powerful, cost-effective microcontroller with Wi-Fi connectivity.
  - **Raspberry Pi**: While technically a single-board computer, it's often used in IoT applications for more powerful tasks.

Communication Protocols for IoT:

- IoT devices use a variety of communication protocols to connect to the internet and other devices. These protocols allow microcontrollers to transmit data to the cloud or communicate with other devices in real-time.

- o **Wi-Fi:** Ideal for home and office IoT projects that require reliable, high-speed internet connections.
- o **Bluetooth:** Useful for low-power, short-range applications (e.g., wearable devices, smart home systems).
- o **LoRa (Long Range):** Used for long-range, low-power IoT devices, particularly in agricultural or industrial applications.
- o **Zigbee & Z-Wave:** Wireless mesh protocols ideal for smart home systems.

2. Building a Simple IoT Device

In this section, we'll create a simple IoT device using a **microcontroller** to monitor **room temperature** and send the data to a cloud-based platform (such as **ThingSpeak** or **Firebase**) for storage and visualization.

Hardware Requirements:

- **Microcontroller**: ESP32 or ESP8266 (with built-in Wi-Fi)
- **Temperature Sensor**: DHT11 or DHT22 (common temperature and humidity sensor)
- **Cloud Platform**: ThingSpeak (free IoT cloud platform)

- **Jumper wires and breadboard**: For connecting the sensor to the microcontroller.

Software Requirements:

- **Arduino IDE**: A popular platform for writing and uploading code to microcontrollers.
- **Libraries**:
  - **DHT sensor library**: To interface with the DHT11 or DHT22 sensor.
  - **Wi-Fi library**: To connect the microcontroller to the internet.
  - **ThingSpeak library**: To send data to ThingSpeak or another IoT platform.

Step-by-Step Guide:

1. **Connect the DHT sensor**:
   - Connect the **VCC** and **GND** pins of the DHT sensor to the 3.3V and GND pins of the microcontroller.
   - Connect the **data** pin to a GPIO pin on the microcontroller (e.g., GPIO 4).
2. **Install the required libraries**:
   - Open the **Arduino IDE**, and go to **Sketch > Include Library > Manage Libraries**.
   - Install the **DHT sensor library** and **ThingSpeak library**.

3. **Write the code**:

   o The code will:

      ▪ Connect the microcontroller to a Wi-Fi network.

      ▪ Read the temperature and humidity from the DHT sensor.

      ▪ Send the data to ThingSpeak every minute.

c

```
#include <WiFi.h>
#include <ThingSpeak.h>
#include <DHT.h>

// Define your Wi-Fi credentials
const char* ssid = "your_SSID";
const char* password = "your_PASSWORD";

// ThingSpeak Channel Settings
unsigned long channelID = your_channel_ID;
const char * writeAPIKey = "your_API_key";

// DHT Sensor Setup
#define DHTPIN 4
#define DHTTYPE DHT11
DHT dht(DHTPIN, DHTTYPE);

WiFiClient client;
```

```c
void setup() {
Serial.begin(115200);
WiFi.begin(ssid, password);

while (WiFi.status() != WL_CONNECTED) {
  delay(1000);
  Serial.println("Connecting to WiFi...");
}

ThingSpeak.begin(client); // Initialize ThingSpeak
dht.begin(); // Initialize DHT sensor
}

void loop() {
// Read temperature and humidity
float temp = dht.readTemperature();
float humidity = dht.readHumidity();

if (isnan(temp) || isnan(humidity)) {
  Serial.println("Failed to read from DHT sensor!");
  return;
}

// Print to serial monitor for debugging
Serial.print("Temperature: ");
Serial.print(temp);
Serial.print(" °C, Humidity: ");
Serial.print(humidity);
Serial.println(" %");
```

```
// Send data to ThingSpeak
ThingSpeak.setField(1, temp);
ThingSpeak.setField(2, humidity);
ThingSpeak.writeFields(channelID, writeAPIKey);

// Wait for 20 seconds before sending next data
delay(20000);
}
```

4. **Upload the code**:
   o After connecting the microcontroller to your computer, select the appropriate board (e.g., ESP32) and upload the code via the **Arduino IDE**.

5. **Monitor Data on ThingSpeak**:
   o Once the device is connected to Wi-Fi and sending data to ThingSpeak, you can monitor the data in real-time via the ThingSpeak website. You can also visualize the temperature and humidity data using graphs.

---

3. Enhancing the IoT Device

Once you've completed the basic IoT temperature monitoring device, there are many ways to enhance the functionality, including:

- **Adding Multiple Sensors**: Interface other sensors like a pressure sensor or light sensor to monitor multiple parameters.

- **Integrating with Mobile Apps**: Use platforms like **Blynk** or **Adafruit IO** to send data to mobile devices for real-time monitoring.

- **Power Optimization**: Use low-power modes to extend the battery life of your IoT device, especially if it's deployed in remote areas.

- **Security**: Implement encryption (e.g., TLS/SSL) to secure data transmission between the device and the cloud.

:

In this chapter, we covered the basics of **IoT** and how **microcontrollers** play a crucial role in the development of smart, connected devices. We explored a practical example of building a temperature and humidity monitoring IoT device using the **ESP32** microcontroller and **ThingSpeak** as the cloud platform. By the end of this chapter, you should have a solid understanding of how to develop your own IoT devices for various applications, ranging from home automation to industrial monitoring systems.

Chapter 16: Real-Time Operating Systems (RTOS) Basics

In embedded systems, timing and precision are often critical. This is where a **Real-Time Operating System (RTOS)** comes into play. Unlike general-purpose operating systems (GPOS) like Windows or Linux, which are designed to handle a wide variety of tasks with no strict timing guarantees, an RTOS is specifically designed to meet the timing constraints of real-time applications. In this chapter, we will dive into the basics of RTOS, explore **FreeRTOS**—a popular, open-source RTOS for embedded systems—and demonstrate its practical usage with real-world examples.

---

1. What is an RTOS?

Understanding the Need for an RTOS in Embedded Systems:

- Embedded systems often need to handle multiple tasks simultaneously while adhering to strict timing constraints. For example, in a **medical device**, certain tasks—such as monitoring a patient's vital signs—must occur at regular intervals to ensure safety. In this scenario, **task prioritization**, **precise timing**, and **guaranteed response times** are essential.

- An **RTOS** provides these guarantees by managing the execution of tasks, ensuring that time-sensitive operations are executed within a specified time window. It achieves this by using task scheduling, interrupt handling, and various synchronization mechanisms.

Key Differences Between an RTOS and a General-Purpose Operating System:

- **Task Management:** A GPOS uses a scheduler that focuses on fairness and responsiveness across multiple applications, whereas an RTOS prioritizes tasks based on deadlines, urgency, and importance, often using deterministic scheduling algorithms.
- **Timing and Response:** RTOSs are **deterministic**, meaning they can guarantee a response within a specific timeframe, while GPOSs may exhibit unpredictable latencies.
- **Resource Allocation:** In RTOS, resources like CPU time, memory, and I/O devices are allocated based on real-time constraints, ensuring high-priority tasks have the necessary resources to meet deadlines.

---

2. Using FreeRTOS in Embedded Systems
What is FreeRTOS?

- **FreeRTOS** is an open-source RTOS designed for small microcontrollers and embedded systems. It is widely used due to its lightweight nature, scalability, and ease of use. It provides essential real-time capabilities, such as **task scheduling**, **interrupt handling**, and **inter-task communication**, making it ideal for embedded applications that require real-time performance.

Key Features of FreeRTOS:

- **Task Scheduling:** FreeRTOS manages tasks based on their priorities and guarantees timely execution of critical tasks.
- **Semaphores and Mutexes:** These synchronization mechanisms are used to manage access to shared resources, preventing race conditions and ensuring proper task coordination.
- **Queues and Message Buffers:** These allow tasks to send and receive data safely, ensuring smooth communication between different parts of the system.
- **Tickless Mode:** FreeRTOS can operate in a low-power mode where the system clock is only active when needed, helping conserve power in battery-operated devices.

FreeRTOS Architecture Overview:

- The kernel of FreeRTOS manages all the tasks, prioritizes them, and schedules them for execution.

- The **idle task** runs when no other tasks are ready to run.
- **Interrupts** are used to trigger tasks with higher priority.

Setting Up FreeRTOS in Embedded Systems:

- To use FreeRTOS in embedded systems, you'll need to configure the FreeRTOS kernel to run on your specific hardware. This often involves:
  - Initializing the **RTOS kernel**.
  - Defining **tasks**, their priorities, and their functions.
  - Configuring **interrupt service routines** (ISRs) to trigger tasks.
  - Setting up **system clocks** and timers to control task execution time.

---

3. Real-World Example: Implementing a Simple Task Scheduler Using FreeRTOS
Scenario: Building a Simple Task Scheduler

- Imagine you are developing a system that performs two critical tasks:
  1. **Task A**: Reads sensor data every 100 milliseconds.
  2. **Task B**: Controls an LED every 500 milliseconds.

Steps:

1. **Define the Tasks:**
   - o Task A should be scheduled to run at a high priority, as it needs to read sensor data frequently.
   - o Task B should run with a lower priority, as controlling the LED is less time-sensitive.

2. **Configure FreeRTOS:**
   - o Initialize FreeRTOS, set up system timers, and configure interrupt handling.
   - o Define **tasks** using FreeRTOS's xTaskCreate function. Assign priorities and specify the function each task should execute.

3. **Task Synchronization:**
   - o Use **queues** or **semaphores** if tasks need to share data or resources.
   - o Implement **delays** using the FreeRTOS delay function (vTaskDelay()) to ensure tasks run at the right intervals.

4. **Task Scheduling and Execution:**
   - o When the system is powered on, the **RTOS scheduler** will begin executing the tasks based on their priority and timing requirements.
   - o The scheduler will guarantee that Task A executes every 100 milliseconds, while Task B runs every 500 milliseconds, without either task missing its deadline.

4. Example Code (C with FreeRTOS)

c

```c
#include "FreeRTOS.h"
#include "task.h"

// Task A: Read sensor data every 100ms
void vTaskSensor(void *pvParameters) {
  for (;;) {
    // Code to read sensor data
    printf("Reading sensor data...\n");
    vTaskDelay(pdMS_TO_TICKS(100)); // Delay for 100ms
  }
}

// Task B: Control LED every 500ms
void vTaskLEDControl(void *pvParameters) {
  for (;;) {
    // Code to control LED
    printf("Controlling LED...\n");
    vTaskDelay(pdMS_TO_TICKS(500)); // Delay for 500ms
  }
}

int main(void) {
  // Initialize FreeRTOS
  xTaskCreate(vTaskSensor, "Sensor Task", configMINIMAL_STACK_SIZE, NULL, 1, NULL);
```

```
xTaskCreate(vTaskLEDControl,        "LED        Control        Task",
configMINIMAL_STACK_SIZE, NULL, 2, NULL);

    // Start scheduler
    vTaskStartScheduler();

    // Program should never reach here
    for (;;) {}
}
```

5. *Advanced FreeRTOS Concepts*

As you gain experience with FreeRTOS, you'll encounter more advanced concepts like **task communication**, **real-time clocks**, **time-sensitive scheduling**, and **inter-process communication (IPC)**. These can be essential for complex applications, such as industrial automation or advanced robotics.

- **Time-Partitioning:** How FreeRTOS manages multiple tasks based on different deadlines and priorities, ensuring the most critical tasks are always given time on the CPU.
- **Message Queues:** Sending data between tasks safely and synchronously.
- **Inter-task Synchronization:** Using semaphores and mutexes to avoid race conditions.

This chapter introduced the **concepts** of real-time systems and provided an overview of how to implement a **real-time operating system** using **FreeRTOS** in embedded systems. You now have the basic knowledge to set up FreeRTOS, configure tasks, and build real-time applications where timing and synchronization are crucial.

In the next chapter, we will explore **debugging embedded systems**, an essential skill for diagnosing and fixing issues in your real-time applications.

Chapter 17: Designing Embedded Systems: From Idea to Hardware

Designing an embedded system is a multifaceted process that combines **software development**, **hardware design**, and **system integration**. The journey from concept to functioning prototype involves careful planning, decision-making, and testing. This chapter will guide you through the key steps involved in designing embedded systems, from initial requirements gathering to selecting the right hardware and testing the final product. Along the way, we'll explore how to approach system design efficiently and provide a **real-world example** of designing an embedded system for a smart home device.

---

1. Steps in Designing Embedded Systems

Designing an embedded system involves several phases, each of which contributes to the overall success of the project. Let's break down the process step-by-step:

a) Requirements Gathering and System Specification:

- Before starting any design work, it's crucial to understand the **requirements** of the system. This involves gathering information on the desired functionality, performance specifications, and constraints (e.g., power consumption, size, environmental factors).

- Questions to consider:
  - o What is the primary function of the device?
  - o What sensors or actuators need to be interfaced with?
  - o Are there real-time constraints (e.g., latency or deadlines)?
  - o What are the physical and environmental constraints (e.g., battery life, temperature range)?

b) High-Level Design:

- Once you understand the requirements, the next step is to create a **high-level design**. This includes selecting the major components of the system (e.g., microcontroller, sensors, power supply, communication modules) and how they will interact.
- Key considerations:
  - o What peripherals are required? (e.g., ADCs, digital I/O pins, communication protocols like UART or I2C)
  - o What software or firmware is needed? (e.g., RTOS, custom libraries)
  - o How will the system be powered? (e.g., battery-powered, USB-powered)

c) Detailed Design:

- In this phase, the system design is refined. You'll make detailed decisions about the microcontroller architecture, pin configuration, and the software structure (e.g., choosing between polling vs. interrupts).
- **Schematics** for the hardware (wiring of components like sensors and actuators) are created, and software modules are outlined.

d) Prototyping:

- After completing the design, it's time to build a **prototype**. This often involves using development boards (e.g., Arduino, STM32, Raspberry Pi) for rapid prototyping, which allows for easy testing and debugging.
- During this phase, focus on implementing the core functionality and testing individual components before integrating them.

e) Testing and Validation:

- Once the prototype is up and running, thorough testing is essential to ensure that the embedded system meets all functional and performance requirements. This includes both **unit testing** (individual components) and **integration testing** (the system as a whole).

- It's important to verify that the system works in the intended environment, particularly if real-time performance or critical functionalities are required.

f) Iteration and Improvement:

- After testing, you may encounter issues such as unexpected behavior, performance bottlenecks, or hardware limitations. The system design may need to be iterated upon to optimize or address these challenges. Testing is an ongoing process.

---

2. Selecting the Right Microcontroller

Selecting the correct **microcontroller (MCU)** is one of the most important decisions in the design process. The MCU determines the system's capabilities and limitations, so it's essential to choose one that matches the project requirements. Key factors to consider when selecting an MCU:

a) Processing Power:

- The **processing power** of the MCU should match the complexity of the tasks it needs to perform. Consider factors like clock speed, number of cores, and memory. For instance, a **low-power, low-frequency** MCU (e.g., STM32, AVR) might be sufficient for simple tasks, whereas more demanding systems (e.g., real-time data processing) might require a **higher-performance MCU**.

b) Memory Requirements:

- **RAM** and **Flash memory** are critical resources. The amount of RAM determines how much data the MCU can process at once, while Flash memory stores your program code.
- For embedded systems with large data or complex algorithms, you may need an MCU with higher memory capacity.

c) I/O and Peripherals:

- **Input/output** capabilities, such as GPIO pins, PWM, ADC/DAC channels, and communication interfaces (UART, SPI, I2C), play an important role in selecting an MCU.
- Consider how many digital and analog inputs/outputs you need and what kind of sensors or actuators will be used in the system.

d) Power Consumption:

- If your embedded system needs to operate in **battery-powered** environments, power consumption is a key factor.

Look for MCUs with **low-power modes** that can help extend battery life.

e) Development Tools and Ecosystem:

- Some microcontrollers have better **toolchain support** and more robust libraries than others. For instance, **ARM Cortex-M based MCUs** typically offer excellent support, including IDEs, debuggers, and middleware libraries, which can speed up development.

f) Cost and Availability:

- Finally, **cost** and **availability** must be considered. For mass production, the cost per unit can be critical, so choosing an MCU that fits within your budget while still meeting performance requirements is essential.

---

3. Real-World Example: Designing a Custom Embedded System for a Smart Home Device

To apply the concepts from this chapter, let's walk through a **real-world example**: designing a custom embedded system for a smart home device. In this case, we will design a **smart thermostat** that controls home heating and cooling based on user preferences.

Step 1: Requirements Gathering

- The system needs to monitor temperature and humidity, display readings to a user interface, and control a heating/cooling system.
- The device will be controlled via a mobile app or a physical interface (e.g., buttons or touch display).

Step 2: High-Level Design

- **Microcontroller**: We select an **STM32** MCU with sufficient processing power, analog inputs for sensors, and communication interfaces for the user interface.
- **Sensors**: A **DHT22** sensor for temperature and humidity, and a **relay module** to control the heating/cooling system.
- **User Interface**: A **small LCD display** and a simple button interface for setting the temperature.

Step 3: Detailed Design

- The MCU will interface with the **DHT22 sensor** using an **I2C** protocol, process the data, and display it on an **LCD screen**. The system will have **interrupts** set up to monitor the button presses to adjust the target temperature.

Step 4: Prototyping and Testing

- Once the hardware design is completed, we begin prototyping using an STM32 development board and the necessary peripherals. During this phase, the system is programmed to read sensor data, display it on the screen, and control the relay to turn the heating/cooling system on or off.

Step 5: Iteration and Improvement

- Testing reveals some glitches in the temperature control algorithm, so we make adjustments to the logic and optimize the power management to extend battery life.

Designing embedded systems involves not only understanding the hardware and software components but also how to integrate them efficiently to meet the needs of the application. By following a structured design process—from gathering requirements to selecting the right microcontroller and ultimately testing and iterating on your design—you can create functional and reliable embedded systems for a wide range of applications. Through this chapter, we've covered the essential steps and provided a practical example of designing a custom embedded system, showing how all the concepts come together in a real-world scenario.

Chapter 18: Wireless Communication in Embedded Systems

Wireless communication has become an integral part of modern embedded systems, enabling devices to interact with each other and the internet without the need for physical connections. Whether it's for **IoT applications**, **remote monitoring**, or **smart devices**, wireless communication protocols play a crucial role in facilitating data transfer and system integration.

This chapter will provide a comprehensive overview of wireless communication protocols commonly used in embedded systems. We will also look at how to interface with wireless modules using **C programming** and explore a **real-world example** of building a wireless sensor network for remote monitoring.

---

1. Wireless Protocols

Wireless protocols are essential for communication between embedded systems. There are various protocols, each suited for different types of applications depending on factors like data rate, range, power consumption, and complexity. Here's an overview of the most commonly used wireless communication protocols in embedded systems:

a) Bluetooth:

- **Overview**: Bluetooth is a widely used short-range wireless technology that allows devices to communicate with each other.

- **Use Cases**: Ideal for applications that require low power consumption and short-range communication (e.g., wearable devices, health monitoring systems, and consumer electronics).

- **Versions**: The latest version, **Bluetooth Low Energy (BLE)**, is optimized for low-power devices, making it suitable for battery-operated applications.

b) Zigbee:

- **Overview**: Zigbee is a low-power, low-data-rate wireless protocol based on IEEE 802.15.4 standards, commonly used for building **sensor networks** and **home automation systems**.

- **Use Cases**: Zigbee is often employed in applications where devices need to form a mesh network, such as smart home devices and industrial control systems.

c) Wi-Fi:

- **Overview**: Wi-Fi is a high-speed wireless communication protocol that allows devices to connect to the internet or local networks.

- **Use Cases**: Used in applications that require internet connectivity, such as smart devices, security cameras, and home automation systems. However, it consumes more power than other low-power protocols.

d) LoRa (Long Range):

- **Overview**: LoRa is a long-range, low-power wireless protocol designed for low data-rate, wide-area networks.
- **Use Cases**: LoRa is ideal for remote sensing, agriculture, and industrial IoT applications where long-range communication is required, such as in smart city projects or environmental monitoring.

e) NFC (Near Field Communication):

- **Overview**: NFC is a short-range wireless technology that allows devices to communicate over very short distances (typically less than 10 cm).
- **Use Cases**: NFC is widely used in applications like **contactless payment systems**, **identity verification**, and **access control**.

---

2. Programming Wireless Modules in C

To enable wireless communication in embedded systems, you'll need to interface with specific wireless modules that implement these protocols. In this section, we will look at how to set up and program two popular wireless modules: **ESP8266** (for Wi-Fi communication) and **nRF24L01** (for low-power wireless communication).

a) Setting Up the ESP8266 for Wi-Fi Communication:

- **Overview**: The **ESP8266** is a low-cost Wi-Fi module that can be easily integrated into embedded systems for wireless communication. It is widely used in IoT projects due to its simplicity and low power consumption.

- **Setup**:
    1. Connect the **ESP8266** to the microcontroller using **UART** (Universal Asynchronous Receiver/Transmitter).
    2. Set up the **Wi-Fi library** in C (for example, using **ESP8266WiFi.h** if you're working with the Arduino IDE).
    3. Program the module to connect to a Wi-Fi network and send or receive data.

- **Example Code**: A simple example to connect the ESP8266 to Wi-Fi and print the device's IP address.

c

```
#include <ESP8266WiFi.h>

const char* ssid = "your_network_ssid";
const char* password = "your_network_password";

void setup() {
  Serial.begin(115200);
  WiFi.begin(ssid, password);

  while (WiFi.status() != WL_CONNECTED) {
    delay(500);
    Serial.print(".");
  }

  Serial.println("Connected to WiFi!");
  Serial.print("IP Address: ");
  Serial.println(WiFi.localIP());
}

void loop() {
  // Your application logic here
}
```

b) Setting Up the nRF24L01 for Wireless Communication:

- **Overview**: The **nRF24L01** is a popular wireless module for creating low-power, short-range communication between devices. It operates on the 2.4 GHz ISM band and supports both point-to-point and multi-point communication.

145

- **Setup**:
  1. Connect the **nRF24L01** module to the microcontroller via **SPI** (Serial Peripheral Interface).
  2. Use the **RF24** library (or equivalent) to set up the wireless communication.
- **Example Code**: A simple example of setting up an **nRF24L01** module to send and receive data.

c

```
#include <SPI.h>
#include <nRF24L01.h>
#include <RF24.h>

RF24 radio(9, 10); // CE, CSN pins
const byte address[6] = "00001";

void setup() {
  Serial.begin(9600);
  radio.begin();
  radio.openWritingPipe(address);
  radio.setPALevel(RF24_PA_HIGH);
  radio.setChannel(100);
}

void loop() {
  char text[] = "Hello, Wireless!";
  radio.write(&text, sizeof(text));
  delay(1000);
```

}

---

3. Real-World Example: Building a Wireless Sensor Network for Remote Monitoring

Now that you understand the basics of wireless protocols and how to interface with wireless modules, let's walk through a practical example. We'll design a simple wireless sensor network (WSN) for **remote monitoring** using **nRF24L01** modules to send sensor data (e.g., temperature, humidity) from multiple sensor nodes to a central receiver.

a) System Overview:

- **Sensor Nodes**: Each sensor node consists of a microcontroller (e.g., Arduino) and a **temperature/humidity sensor** (e.g., DHT11/DHT22). The sensor nodes will send data wirelessly via the **nRF24L01** to a central hub.
- **Receiver**: The central hub will receive data from the sensor nodes, process the data, and display it on a local LCD screen or send it to a cloud service via Wi-Fi.

b) Components:

- **Microcontroller**: Arduino (or any microcontroller with SPI support)

- **Wireless Module**: nRF24L01
- **Sensors**: DHT11 or DHT22 (for temperature and humidity)
- **Power Supply**: Battery-powered for sensor nodes and USB-powered for the receiver

c) Implementation:

- **Sensor Node Code**: The sensor node reads temperature and humidity from the sensor and transmits the data to the receiver.
- **Receiver Code**: The receiver listens for incoming data and displays it on an LCD screen or processes it further (e.g., uploading to the cloud).

This example illustrates how to build a simple, wireless **sensor network** that can be expanded to monitor various environmental parameters over a larger area.

By the end of this chapter, you will have gained hands-on experience with programming wireless communication modules in C and will be able to build a range of wireless systems, from simple point-to-point communication setups to more complex sensor networks. Whether you're working on **IoT projects** or building **remote control systems**, wireless communication will be a crucial skill for your embedded systems projects.

Chapter 19: Embedded System Security

In today's interconnected world, the security of embedded systems is of paramount importance. Embedded systems, which are integrated into various devices ranging from industrial machines to everyday consumer electronics, are often vulnerable to attacks due to their limited resources and exposure to the internet or other networks. With the rise of the **Internet of Things (IoT)**, ensuring that embedded systems are secure is more critical than ever.

This chapter will dive into the unique security challenges faced by embedded systems, explore some basic but essential security measures, and guide you through a **real-world example** of implementing security features in an embedded communication system.

---

1. Security Challenges in Embedded Systems

Embedded systems are inherently vulnerable to a variety of security threats due to their limited resources (e.g., processing power, memory), exposed communication channels, and integration with other devices or networks. Some of the primary security challenges faced by embedded systems include:

a) Lack of Security Updates:

- Many embedded systems are deployed with limited or no means to apply security updates once they are in the field. This makes them highly vulnerable to exploits as new vulnerabilities are discovered.

b) Physical Attacks:

- Attackers may gain physical access to embedded systems, which can lead to reverse engineering or direct manipulation of the device.

c) Network-Based Attacks:

- As more embedded devices become part of the Internet of Things (IoT), they are exposed to a broader set of network-based attacks, such as man-in-the-middle (MITM) attacks, denial-of-service (DoS) attacks, and eavesdropping on unsecured communication.

d) Inadequate Cryptography:

- Many embedded systems are either underprotected or have weak cryptographic implementations, which can be easily cracked by attackers.

e) Resource Constraints:

- Embedded systems have limited processing power, memory, and storage, which can hinder the implementation of security measures like strong encryption or complex authentication methods.

---

2. Basic Security Measures

While embedded systems may be resource-constrained, there are several effective and relatively simple security techniques that can be implemented to protect against common threats. The following are some fundamental security measures for embedded systems:

a) Encryption:

- **Purpose**: Encryption ensures that sensitive data (such as passwords or communication messages) cannot be intercepted and read by unauthorized parties.
- **Implementation**: Even with limited resources, lightweight encryption algorithms like **AES (Advanced Encryption Standard)** or **ECC (Elliptic Curve Cryptography)** can be used to secure data in transit or at rest.
- **Example**: Encrypting data sent over a wireless communication protocol like **Bluetooth** or **Wi-Fi** using symmetric or asymmetric encryption.

b) Secure Boot:

- **Purpose**: Secure boot ensures that a device only boots from trusted, authenticated firmware. This prevents attackers from loading malicious code or firmware during the boot process.
- **Implementation**: During boot, the system checks the integrity of the firmware using a cryptographic signature. If the signature doesn't match, the system refuses to boot, preventing the execution of unauthorized code.

c) Secure Communication:

- **Purpose**: Ensuring that communication between devices is encrypted and authenticated helps to protect against eavesdropping and spoofing attacks.
- **Implementation**: For secure communication, use **TLS (Transport Layer Security)** or **SSL (Secure Sockets Layer)** protocols, which provide encryption and integrity protection for data sent over networks. Alternatively, simpler encryption protocols like **AES-128** can be used in constrained environments.

d) Authentication and Authorization:

- **Purpose**: Authenticating users and devices ensures that only authorized entities can access or control an embedded system.

- **Implementation**: Use **password-based authentication**, **two-factor authentication (2FA)**, or **public key infrastructure (PKI)** for devices. For more resource-constrained devices, **shared secret keys** or **hardware security modules (HSMs)** can be used.

e) Firmware Integrity Checking:

- **Purpose**: This method ensures that the firmware running on an embedded system has not been tampered with.
- **Implementation**: Implement periodic checks to verify the integrity of the firmware using hash-based verification or digital signatures. If the firmware has been altered, the system can either self-repair or notify the user.

---

3. Real-World Example: Implementing Simple Encryption for a Remote Communication System

Let's implement a simple encryption scheme for a remote communication system between two microcontrollers. For the sake of simplicity, we'll use a **symmetric encryption** algorithm like **AES-128**, which is both secure and efficient for embedded systems. This will involve encrypting data before it is transmitted and decrypting it upon receipt.

Step 1: Choose the Encryption Algorithm

- Use **AES-128** for symmetric encryption. We'll need to install a lightweight library like **mbedTLS** or use **Arduino's AES library** for small microcontrollers.

Step 2: Set Up the Communication Channel

- Establish a UART or SPI communication channel between two microcontrollers.

Step 3: Encrypt Data Before Transmission

- Before sending any data, use the encryption function to convert the plain-text data into cipher-text.

Step 4: Transmit the Encrypted Data

- Send the encrypted data over the UART or SPI communication interface.

Step 5: Decrypt Data on the Receiver Side

- Upon receiving the encrypted data, use the corresponding decryption function to retrieve the original plain-text data.

Code Example (Simplified Pseudo-C Code for AES Encryption):

c

```c
#include <aes.h>  // Include the AES library

void encryptData(uint8_t* data, uint8_t* key, uint8_t* encryptedData) {
    AES_CTX ctx;
    AES_init_ctx(&ctx, key);  // Initialize AES context with key
    AES_encrypt(&ctx, data, encryptedData);  // Encrypt the data
}

void decryptData(uint8_t* encryptedData, uint8_t* key, uint8_t* decryptedData) {
    AES_CTX ctx;
    AES_init_ctx(&ctx, key);  // Initialize AES context with key
    AES_decrypt(&ctx, encryptedData, decryptedData);  // Decrypt the data
}
```

Step 6: Securely Store Keys

- Store encryption keys in a secure manner, possibly using the microcontroller's **secure storage** feature (e.g., EEPROM or external memory).

Embedded system security is an essential aspect of the design and development process. While embedded devices are resource-constrained, employing fundamental security measures like encryption, secure boot, and secure communication can go a long way in safeguarding these devices from malicious attacks. By applying the techniques discussed in this chapter, you will be better equipped to protect your embedded systems from security threats in real-world applications.

Chapter 20: Software and Firmware Updates in Embedded Systems

Embedded systems are often deployed in environments where direct access is difficult or impossible, such as in remote sensors, industrial machinery, or consumer IoT devices. These systems need regular updates to fix bugs, patch security vulnerabilities, improve performance, or add new features. Without a reliable method to update software or firmware, embedded devices can become outdated or compromised over time. This chapter explores the **importance of software and firmware updates**, how to implement **Over-the-Air (OTA) updates**, and a **real-world example** of creating a firmware update system for a smart device.

---

1. Why Updates Matter

Software and firmware updates are critical for maintaining the security, functionality, and longevity of embedded systems. The need for regular updates arises from several factors:

a) Bug Fixes and Performance Enhancements:

- Like any software, embedded system firmware may have bugs or performance bottlenecks that need to be addressed. These bugs can range from minor glitches to critical issues that impact system stability.

- Regular updates allow developers to fix these issues, improving the system's overall performance and reliability.

b) Security Vulnerabilities:

- Embedded systems, especially those connected to the internet (e.g., IoT devices), are prime targets for cyber-attacks. Hackers can exploit security vulnerabilities in outdated firmware, compromising the system and potentially gaining control.
- Security patches via updates are crucial to close these vulnerabilities and protect the system from potential breaches.

c) Feature Enhancements and Upgrades:

- As technology evolves, new features or protocols may become available that can enhance the functionality of embedded systems.
- Updates allow systems to stay current with the latest advancements, providing users with new features without the need for hardware upgrades.

d) Compliance with Standards:

- Embedded systems, particularly in industries like automotive or healthcare, must comply with strict regulatory standards.
- Software updates can be used to ensure the system meets the latest compliance standards or industry best practices.

---

2. Methods for Over-the-Air (OTA) Updates

Over-the-Air (OTA) updates are a popular method for updating the software or firmware of embedded systems remotely, without requiring physical access to the device. OTA updates are especially useful for devices deployed in the field, such as IoT sensors, remote control systems, and industrial machines.

a) Types of OTA Updates:

a.1) Incremental Updates:

- Only the changes or differences (deltas) between the current firmware and the new version are transmitted. This saves bandwidth and makes the update process faster.

a.2) Full Image Updates:

- The entire firmware image is sent to the device, which replaces the old firmware completely. Although this approach uses more bandwidth, it ensures the device gets the complete, most up-to-date version.

b) OTA Update Process:

b.1) Secure Communication:

- The first step in OTA updates is ensuring secure communication between the device and the update server. Protocols such as **HTTPS** or **MQTT** can be used to securely transfer the update files.
- Encryption of the firmware file ensures that the update process cannot be intercepted or tampered with.

b.2) Version Checking:

- Before initiating an update, the embedded system checks the version of the firmware it is currently running and compares it to the version available on the server.
- If the available version is newer, the update process proceeds; otherwise, the system does nothing.

b.3) Downloading the Update:

- Once a valid update is detected, the system downloads the update file. The download can be done in a way that the device continues to operate while the update is being downloaded (non-blocking).

b.4) Flashing the Firmware:

- After downloading, the device writes the new firmware to its flash memory. During this process, the device may temporarily enter a **safe mode** to ensure the firmware is updated correctly.
- Some devices use a **dual-bank system**, where the old firmware is preserved on one bank of memory, and the new firmware is written to the other. If the update fails, the system can fall back on the old firmware.

b.5) Verification:

- After the firmware is flashed, the system must verify that the update was successful. This could involve checking the firmware's integrity using checksums or hash functions to confirm that the new firmware is valid and uncorrupted.

c) Error Handling and Rollback:

- A robust error-handling mechanism is crucial for OTA updates. If the update process fails, the system should automatically revert to the previous firmware version to avoid bricking the device.
- In some systems, the bootloader can handle rollback functionality, ensuring that even if the new firmware fails to load, the device can still recover using a backup.

3. Real-World Example: Creating a Firmware Update System for a Smart Device

To demonstrate how OTA updates are implemented, let's consider a **smart thermostat** that controls heating and cooling in a home. This device needs to update its firmware regularly to enhance its features, fix bugs, or patch security vulnerabilities.

Step 1: Setting Up the Firmware Update Server

- We begin by setting up a secure server where the latest firmware versions are stored. The server must support secure protocols (e.g., **HTTPS**) to ensure the communication between the device and the server is encrypted.
- A simple database can be used to track the current version of the firmware installed on each device and to store new firmware releases.

Step 2: Configuring the Smart Thermostat for OTA Updates

- The thermostat is equipped with Wi-Fi capabilities, allowing it to connect to the internet. It can communicate with the firmware update server using the **HTTP** protocol.
- The thermostat is programmed to periodically check for available updates by sending a request to the update server.

Step 3: Version Checking and Downloading the Update

- Once the thermostat detects that a new firmware version is available, it verifies that the version number is higher than the current one.
- The thermostat downloads the update file in an incremental or full-image format, depending on the update type.

Step 4: Firmware Flashing and Verification

- The thermostat enters a safe mode while it flashes the new firmware into its flash memory. After the flashing process, it performs a verification check to ensure the firmware is correct and the update was successful.
- If the verification fails, the thermostat can roll back to the previous firmware using a backup stored in a secondary memory bank.

Step 5: Final Verification and Reboot

- Once the update is successfully installed and verified, the thermostat reboots with the new firmware, and the system becomes operational again.
- If needed, additional checks can be performed to ensure that the thermostat operates correctly after the update.

Software and firmware updates are an essential part of maintaining and improving embedded systems. With Over-the-Air (OTA) updates, developers can easily update devices deployed in the field, improving functionality, patching vulnerabilities, and enhancing performance. The implementation of secure, reliable, and efficient update systems ensures that embedded devices remain useful and secure throughout their lifecycle. This chapter provided an in-depth look at how firmware updates are implemented in embedded systems and included a practical example to help you understand the process.

Chapter 21: Integrating Embedded Systems with Cloud Platforms

In the modern world of **Internet of Things (IoT)**, integrating embedded systems with cloud platforms has become a pivotal aspect of advancing data-driven decision-making, remote monitoring, and real-time analysis. By connecting embedded systems to the cloud, engineers can leverage the vast computational power, storage capabilities, and data analytics tools provided by cloud platforms like **AWS (Amazon Web Services)**, **Google Cloud**, and others. This chapter delves into the **process of connecting embedded systems to cloud platforms**, explores **communication protocols**, and provides a **real-world example** of building a cloud-connected weather station using a microcontroller.

---

1. Connecting Embedded Systems to the Cloud
a) Cloud Platforms for Embedded Systems:

- Cloud platforms provide the infrastructure and services that allow embedded systems to send data for storage, processing, and analysis. Some of the popular cloud platforms include:

o **AWS IoT Core**: A managed cloud service that allows you to securely connect devices to the cloud and other AWS services.

o **Google Cloud IoT**: A set of fully managed services that help connect, manage, and analyze IoT data.

o **Microsoft Azure IoT**: Provides a suite of services for building and managing IoT applications.

o **IBM Watson IoT**: A cloud service offering device management, real-time data processing, and analytics.

b) Communication Protocols:

- Embedded systems typically communicate with cloud platforms over the internet using lightweight communication protocols. These protocols are designed to be low bandwidth, secure, and optimized for small devices.

    o **MQTT (Message Queuing Telemetry Transport)**: A lightweight messaging protocol used widely in IoT applications for transmitting data between devices and cloud services.

    o **HTTP/HTTPS**: Common web protocols used to send data to cloud services.

    o **CoAP (Constrained Application Protocol)**: A lightweight protocol designed for constrained devices, ideal for low-power systems.

     o **WebSockets**: Used for establishing a continuous connection between the embedded device and the cloud.

c) Data Collection and Analytics:

- Cloud platforms not only collect data but also provide powerful tools for processing and analyzing it. For example:
  - **Data Lakes** and **Databases**: Cloud platforms can store vast amounts of sensor data.
  - **Data Analytics Tools**: Platforms like AWS and Google Cloud offer machine learning and data analysis tools that can be applied to sensor data to detect patterns, predict trends, and provide actionable insights.

---

2. Real-World Example: Building a Cloud-Connected Weather Station with a Microcontroller

Let's walk through a real-world example where we build a simple weather station using an embedded system that collects weather data and sends it to a cloud platform for storage and analysis. This example will demonstrate the complete process of **sensor integration, data transmission, and cloud analytics**.

Step 1: Selecting the Hardware

- **Microcontroller**: A common microcontroller used for IoT applications, such as the **ESP32** or **Arduino**, can be used to collect data from sensors.

- **Sensors**: For this example, a **DHT22** sensor (for temperature and humidity) and a **BMP180** sensor (for pressure and altitude) can be used to collect environmental data.

- **Cloud Platform**: We will use **AWS IoT Core** to manage the devices and store the data.

- **Connectivity**: The **ESP32** microcontroller comes with built-in **Wi-Fi**, allowing it to connect to the internet and transmit data.

Step 2: Setting Up the Cloud Platform

- Create an **AWS IoT Core account** and set up a new IoT thing (representing the weather station device).

- Generate security credentials (such as an **X.509 certificate**) to ensure secure communication between the microcontroller and AWS IoT.

- Set up a **topic** in AWS to receive data from the weather station. For example, weather_station/data.

Step 3: Programming the Microcontroller

- Write a program in **C/C++** or **Arduino IDE** to read data from the sensors.

- Use **Wi-Fi** to connect the microcontroller to the internet.
- Use **MQTT** to send data to the cloud platform. This involves setting up an MQTT client on the microcontroller and configuring it to publish sensor readings to the AWS IoT Core topic.

Example Code Snippet:

cpp

```cpp
#include <WiFi.h>
#include <PubSubClient.h>

WiFiClient wifiClient;
PubSubClient client(wifiClient);

const char* ssid = "your_SSID";
const char* password = "your_PASSWORD";
const char* mqttServer = "your_AWS_IoT_endpoint";

void setup() {
  Serial.begin(115200);

  // Connect to Wi-Fi
  WiFi.begin(ssid, password);
  while (WiFi.status() != WL_CONNECTED) {
    delay(1000);
    Serial.print(".");
  }
  Serial.println("Connected to Wi-Fi");
```

```
// Connect to MQTT
client.setServer(mqttServer, 8883);   // AWS IoT uses port 8883 for secure
MQTT
while (!client.connected()) {
  if (client.connect("weather_station")) {
    Serial.println("Connected to AWS IoT");
  } else {
    delay(5000);
  }
 }
}

void loop() {
  // Read sensor data (temperature, humidity, etc.)
  float temperature = readTemperature(); // Replace with actual sensor code
  float humidity = readHumidity();       // Replace with actual sensor code

  // Create JSON payload
  String payload = "{\"temperature\": " + String(temperature) + ", \"humidity\": "
+ String(humidity) + "}";

  // Publish data to AWS IoT
  client.publish("weather_station/data", payload.c_str());

  delay(60000);  // Wait for 1 minute before sending next data
}

float readTemperature() {
  // Replace with actual code to read from temperature sensor
```

```
  return 25.0;  // Example static value
}
```

```
float readHumidity() {
  // Replace with actual code to read from humidity sensor
  return 60.0;  // Example static value
}
```

Step 4: Visualizing Data in the Cloud

- Use **AWS IoT Analytics** or **AWS QuickSight** to visualize the incoming weather data.
- You can create dashboards to monitor the temperature, humidity, and pressure readings in real time.
- Set up alerts based on certain thresholds (e.g., if temperature exceeds 30°C).

Step 5: Analyzing Data

- With the data stored in the cloud, you can now apply data analytics, such as predicting weather patterns, correlating temperature and humidity, or detecting anomalies.

Integrating embedded systems with cloud platforms is a powerful technique for extending the capabilities of embedded systems. By connecting sensors and devices to cloud services like **AWS**,

Google Cloud, or **Microsoft Azure**, engineers can create intelligent, data-driven solutions. In this chapter, we built a **cloud-connected weather station**, which not only monitors environmental conditions but also leverages cloud storage and analytics to gain insights and make informed decisions. The principles and techniques discussed here can be applied to a wide range of applications, from **industrial IoT** to **smart homes** and **environmental monitoring** systems.

Chapter 22: Safety and Reliability in Embedded Systems

Safety and reliability are paramount in embedded systems, especially when these systems are used in critical applications such as medical devices, automotive systems, aerospace, industrial control, and more. In these areas, failures can lead to severe consequences, including loss of life, environmental harm, or substantial economic costs. Therefore, engineers must design embedded systems with robust safety measures, redundancy, and fault tolerance to ensure that they continue to operate correctly, even under extreme conditions or in the event of partial failure.

In this chapter, we will explore techniques for designing **safe and reliable embedded systems**, including **redundancy**, **fail-safes**, **testing**, and **validation**. We will also present a **real-world example** of building a fail-safe system for an industrial application, where safety and reliability are critical.

---

1. Designing for Safety

a) Redundancy in Embedded Systems:

- **Redundancy** involves the inclusion of additional components or systems to back up the primary system in

case of failure. There are several types of redundancy that can be applied in embedded system design:

- o **Hardware Redundancy**: This includes duplicating critical hardware components (e.g., processors, power supplies) to ensure the system remains functional if one component fails.

- o **Software Redundancy**: Redundant software routines or safety-critical algorithms can be implemented to detect errors or take over in case of failures.

- o **Data Redundancy**: Storing multiple copies of data or using error-correction codes (ECC) to prevent data corruption or loss.

- • **Example**: In aerospace systems, **dual-redundant flight control systems** are common. If one system fails, the other can take over without loss of control.

b) Fail-Safes and Safety Mechanisms:

- • A **fail-safe** system is designed to bring the system into a safe state in case of a failure, minimizing the risk of harm. For instance, embedded systems can be programmed to shut down or switch to backup systems if they detect a critical failure.

- o **Watchdog Timers**: A watchdog timer ensures that if a system crashes or freezes, it can automatically reset or enter a safe state.

- o **Self-Testing**: Embedded systems can perform built-in self-tests (BIST) to ensure that the system is operating within expected parameters.

- **Example**: In medical devices, a **fail-safe shutdown** is employed to stop operations if the system detects abnormal readings or malfunctions that could pose a risk to patient safety.

c) Designing for Fault Tolerance:

- **Fault tolerance** refers to the ability of a system to continue operating correctly even when a part of the system fails. Embedded systems can be made fault-tolerant by incorporating redundancy, error-checking algorithms, and backup components.

  - o **Error Detection and Correction (EDAC)**: Techniques like **parity checks**, **checksums**, and **Cyclic Redundancy Checks (CRC)** help identify errors in data transmission and storage, allowing the system to detect and correct them.

  - o **Graceful Degradation**: Instead of failing completely, some embedded systems are designed

to continue operation at reduced capacity when certain components fail.

- **Example**: In **industrial control systems**, a **redundant power supply** ensures that if one power source fails, the other takes over without system interruption.

---

2. *Ensuring System Reliability*

a) Testing and Validation of Embedded Systems:

- To ensure the reliability of an embedded system, rigorous **testing** and **validation** are required. This involves checking the system's behavior under normal and extreme conditions to ensure it performs as expected.

  o **Unit Testing**: Testing individual components or modules of the system to ensure they function correctly.

  o **Integration Testing**: Verifying that different parts of the system work together as intended.

  o **Stress Testing**: Subjecting the system to extreme conditions (e.g., high temperatures, high voltage, overclocking) to verify its robustness.

- **Example**: In **automotive systems**, safety-critical components like **airbag control units** undergo extensive

fault injection testing to simulate real-world failures and ensure they function correctly under all conditions.

b) Reliability Metrics:

- Engineers often use specific **reliability metrics** to evaluate the performance and longevity of embedded systems:
    - **Mean Time Between Failures (MTBF)**: The average time a system operates before it fails. High MTBF values indicate high reliability.
    - **Failure Modes and Effects Analysis (FMEA)**: A systematic method for evaluating potential failure modes of a system and assessing their impact on the overall performance.
    - **Reliability Block Diagrams (RBD)**: A graphical representation of a system's components and their reliability interdependencies.
- **Example**: In **medical devices**, achieving a high MTBF is crucial for ensuring continuous operation and avoiding failures that could impact patient health.

c) Formal Verification Methods:

- Formal verification involves mathematically proving that a system behaves as intended under all possible conditions. This is particularly important in safety-critical applications like **automotive, aerospace**, and **medical devices**.

- o **Model Checking**: A method used to verify that a system's behavior satisfies the desired properties by exhaustively exploring all possible states of the system.

- o **Static Code Analysis**: Automated tools that analyze source code without executing it to detect potential errors, vulnerabilities, or inefficiencies.

- **Example**: In **aerospace**, **formal verification** is used to ensure that embedded systems controlling aircraft navigation adhere to strict safety standards.

---

3. Real-World Example: Building a Fail-Safe System for an Industrial Application

Let's put the concepts of safety and reliability into practice with a real-world example: **designing a fail-safe system for an industrial automation application**.

Scenario:

- In an industrial facility, a **robotic arm** is responsible for moving heavy machinery parts. The robot is controlled by an embedded system, and safety is crucial to prevent accidents.

Designing the System:

1. **Redundancy**: The system uses two independent microcontrollers to control the robotic arm, ensuring that if one microcontroller fails, the other can take over.

2. **Watchdog Timer**: A watchdog timer is employed to monitor the robot's status. If the robot becomes unresponsive, the watchdog timer triggers a reset and ensures the robot enters a safe mode.

3. **Fail-Safe Mechanisms**: The system is designed to automatically stop the robot's motion if any critical sensor fails, such as proximity sensors or load sensors.

4. **Error Checking**: Communication between the microcontrollers is protected with CRC to detect transmission errors.

5. **Fault-Tolerant Power Supply**: The system uses a redundant power supply, ensuring that if one power source fails, the robot will continue operating.

Outcome:

- The fail-safe system ensures that the robotic arm operates with high reliability, even in the presence of faults or failures. The system automatically triggers recovery procedures, minimizing downtime and preventing accidents.

In embedded systems, **safety** and **reliability** are non-negotiable, especially when the systems are used in critical applications such as healthcare, automotive, and industrial control. Through redundancy, fail-safe designs, fault tolerance, testing, and formal verification, engineers can ensure that embedded systems perform optimally, even under harsh or unexpected conditions. By integrating these techniques into the design process, engineers can create robust systems that deliver safe and dependable performance for years to come.

Chapter 23: Advanced Topics in Embedded Systems

As embedded systems become more complex and are increasingly used in demanding applications, it is important to understand and utilize advanced features and techniques to maximize performance, functionality, and efficiency. In this chapter, we will explore some of the **advanced features** and techniques used in embedded systems development, such as **Direct Memory Access (DMA)** and **coprocessors**, as well as **complex peripheral interfaces**. These topics are crucial when designing systems that must handle high data throughput, real-time processing, and multiple complex peripherals.

We will conclude with a **real-world example** demonstrating how to integrate an advanced sensor array with a microcontroller, specifically tailored for an industrial system, showcasing the application of these advanced topics.

---

1. Advanced Microcontroller Features
a) Direct Memory Access (DMA):

- **What is DMA?**
    - **Direct Memory Access (DMA)** is a feature that allows peripherals to transfer data to and from

memory without involving the CPU. This reduces the load on the CPU, enabling faster and more efficient data processing, especially in systems with high throughput requirements.

- **When to Use DMA:**
  - o DMA is particularly useful in applications where large amounts of data need to be moved quickly, such as audio or video processing, data logging, or sensor data collection in real-time systems.

- **How DMA Works:**
  - o DMA channels are configured to handle data transfers between peripherals (e.g., ADCs, sensors) and memory, bypassing the CPU for data transfer. The CPU is only involved in setting up the transfer and handling interrupts once the transfer is complete.

- **Configuring DMA in C:**
  - o Setting up DMA involves configuring registers to enable DMA channels, specify the source and destination addresses, set the transfer direction, and configure interrupt handling for completion.

b) Coprocessors and Hardware Acceleration:

- **What are Coprocessors?**

- o A **coprocessor** is a secondary processor designed to handle specific tasks more efficiently than the main microcontroller. Common coprocessors include **floating-point units (FPUs)**, **signal processing units (DSPs)**, and **cryptographic accelerators**.

- **Applications of Coprocessors:**
  - o Coprocessors are commonly used in applications that involve complex mathematical operations, such as digital signal processing (DSP), encryption, or floating-point calculations.

- **Integrating Coprocessors:**
  - o Coprocessors can be integrated into a microcontroller or connected externally. Integration may involve configuring the coprocessor's registers, setting up communication protocols, and handling interrupts from the coprocessor when it completes its tasks.

---

2. Complex Peripheral Interfaces

a) Interfacing with Advanced Sensors:

- **Sensor Types:**
  - o As embedded systems are used in more advanced applications, engineers need to interface with

complex sensors such as **gas sensors**, **imaging sensors**, **multi-axis accelerometers**, **LIDAR**, and **radar** sensors.

- **Communication Protocols for Sensors:**
  - o Sensors often use advanced communication protocols such as **SPI**, **I2C**, **CAN**, or **RS-485** to send data. Some sensors may also require **DMA** or **high-speed data transfer** to handle large amounts of data.

- **Signal Conditioning:**
  - o Many advanced sensors require **signal conditioning** to convert analog signals to digital or to filter out noise before passing data to the microcontroller.

b) Interfacing with Displays:

- **High-Resolution Displays:**
  - o Embedded systems often interface with **high-resolution TFT**, **OLED**, or **LED displays**. These displays may use **SPI**, **parallel**, or even **LVDS (Low-Voltage Differential Signaling)** for high-speed data transfer.

- **Touchscreen Displays:**
  - o For systems requiring user interaction, **touchscreen interfaces** are integrated into embedded designs. These displays often use **capacitive** or **resistive**

touchscreen technology, with communication protocols like **I2C** or **SPI**.

- **Graphical Libraries:**
  - o Implementing advanced graphics requires efficient programming. Libraries such as **LittlevGL** or **uGFX** allow developers to design user-friendly interfaces.

c) Managing Multiple Peripherals Simultaneously:

- **Multiplexing:**
  - o In systems where there are many sensors or actuators, **multiplexing** may be used to select which peripherals are active at any given time. This allows systems with limited I/O pins to interact with multiple devices.
- **DMA and Multiple Peripherals:**
  - o For systems that involve multiple high-speed peripherals (e.g., sensors, actuators, and displays), **DMA** can be utilized to offload data transfer tasks from the CPU, thus ensuring smooth concurrent operation.

---

3. Real-World Example: Integrating an Advanced Sensor Array with a Microcontroller for an Industrial System

In this example, we will demonstrate how to integrate an **advanced sensor array** consisting of multiple types of sensors (e.g., temperature, humidity, pressure, and motion sensors) with a microcontroller in an **industrial environment**. These sensors will provide real-time data to monitor environmental conditions in a factory or warehouse.

Steps in the Project:

- **Choosing the Right Microcontroller:**
    - Select a microcontroller with adequate **I/O pins**, **communication interfaces** (e.g., **I2C, SPI, UART**), and processing power to handle multiple sensors and control actuators.
- **Sensor Integration:**
    - Connect the sensors to the microcontroller using appropriate communication protocols (e.g., **I2C** for temperature and humidity sensors, **SPI** for motion sensors).
- **Data Collection and Processing:**
    - Use **DMA** to collect data from the sensors and store it in memory efficiently.
    - Implement algorithms to process the sensor data in real-time, such as calculating averages, detecting anomalies, or triggering events when thresholds are reached.

- **Displaying Data and Communication:**
  - Interface the system with a **TFT display** to visualize the data in real-time.
  - Use **UART** or **Wi-Fi** to transmit sensor data to a cloud platform or local server for logging and analysis.
- **Real-Time Control:**
  - Use the data to control industrial equipment, such as fans or HVAC systems, to maintain optimal environmental conditions in the factory.
- **Power Efficiency:**
  - Implement **low-power modes** and **sleep functions** to ensure that the system operates efficiently without draining the power supply.

Outcome:

- The system will continuously monitor environmental conditions, make real-time decisions based on sensor data, and provide feedback through a display. Additionally, it will transmit data to a cloud platform for remote monitoring and analysis.

In this chapter, we covered advanced topics in embedded systems, including **DMA**, **coprocessors**, and **complex peripheral interfaces** such as advanced sensors and displays. These features are essential for building high-performance, efficient, and robust embedded systems in industrial and other critical applications. The real-world example of integrating an advanced sensor array for an industrial system illustrates how these concepts can be applied to practical, real-world challenges.

Chapter 24: Future Trends in Embedded Systems

The field of embedded systems is continuously evolving as new technologies emerge, influencing the way we design, implement, and optimize these systems. In this chapter, we explore some of the **emerging trends** that are shaping the future of embedded systems development, with a particular focus on **artificial intelligence (AI)**, **machine learning (ML)**, and the role of **5G** networks in enhancing system capabilities. Additionally, we will discuss the growing role of **Python** in embedded systems, particularly in the **prototyping** phase and its use for higher-level programming, making embedded systems development more accessible and efficient.

This chapter aims to provide a glimpse into the future, helping engineers and developers understand the direction the embedded systems field is heading and how to stay ahead of the curve.

---

1. Emerging Technologies

a) The Impact of AI and Machine Learning on Embedded Systems:

- **AI and ML Integration:** Artificial Intelligence and Machine Learning are no longer reserved for cloud-based applications. With the increasing computational power of microcontrollers and the availability of efficient algorithms, embedded systems are now being designed to run AI and ML models directly on the device.

- **Edge Computing:** The rise of **edge computing** allows devices to process data locally instead of relying on centralized cloud servers. Embedded systems can make **real-time decisions** based on **sensor data** using ML algorithms, improving responsiveness and reducing latency.

- **Real-World Example:** Smart cameras, such as those used for security or industrial monitoring, can analyze images or video feeds directly on the device to detect objects, faces, or anomalies. Machine learning models trained to recognize patterns can be deployed to microcontrollers to make decisions in real-time.

b) 5G Networks and Their Role in Embedded Systems:

- **High-Speed Connectivity:** 5G is designed to provide ultra-fast data speeds, low latency, and reliable connectivity, enabling embedded systems to function more efficiently and seamlessly within IoT networks. This is particularly useful for systems that require **constant communication** and need to process large volumes of data.

- **Real-Time Remote Monitoring and Control:** 5G connectivity allows embedded systems to be monitored, controlled, and updated remotely with minimal delay. Applications like autonomous vehicles, industrial automation, and remote health monitoring will benefit greatly from the reduced latency and enhanced bandwidth that 5G offers.

- **Real-World Example:** In industrial environments, embedded systems can collect and transmit data from sensors to central servers for analysis in near real-time, supporting **predictive maintenance** and **remote troubleshooting**.

---

2. The Role of Python in Embedded Systems
a) Prototyping with Python:

- **Rapid Development and Testing:** Python is widely known for its ability to facilitate **rapid prototyping**. Its simplicity and large ecosystem of libraries make it an ideal choice for quickly testing and validating embedded systems concepts before moving to low-level languages like C.
- **MicroPython and CircuitPython:** These are lightweight versions of Python designed specifically for microcontrollers. MicroPython runs directly on microcontrollers like the ESP32, STM32, and Raspberry Pi

Pico, allowing developers to write Python code to control hardware, interface with sensors, and manage peripherals.

- **Real-World Example:** A developer can use Python (via MicroPython) to prototype a home automation system on a microcontroller. The system can interface with sensors, motors, and lights, and Python code can be used to rapidly test different algorithms for scheduling and control, significantly accelerating the development process.

b) Python for High-Level Programming:

- **Python as a High-Level Interface:** While C is still the preferred language for low-level embedded programming, Python is increasingly being used for higher-level functions like **user interfaces**, **data processing**, and **network communication**. It provides a clear abstraction over the complex hardware operations and simplifies tasks that do not require direct hardware control.

- **Interfacing Python with C:** In many advanced embedded systems, Python is used to control the system at a high level, while C handles the low-level, performance-critical operations. Python's ability to interface with C libraries makes it easy to develop high-performance embedded applications that are also easy to maintain and extend.

- **Real-World Example:** A smart home device might use Python to interface with a database or cloud service to store and retrieve user preferences, while the microcontroller's main tasks (e.g., controlling lights, processing sensor data) are handled by C. This separation allows for modular design, where Python handles the complexity of higher-level functions and C handles the real-time operations.

: Shaping the Future of Embedded Systems

The future of embedded systems is promising, with AI, machine learning, and 5G networks pushing the boundaries of what these systems can achieve. As embedded devices become smarter and more connected, the ability to process data locally and in real-time will be a key differentiator. Python, once considered more of a tool for high-level applications, is increasingly becoming a vital part of embedded systems development, enabling faster prototyping and simplifying the integration of complex algorithms and cloud connectivity.

As an embedded systems developer, staying up-to-date with these **emerging technologies** and understanding how to leverage **Python** in your projects will be critical to staying competitive in this rapidly evolving field. The tools, libraries, and platforms available today make it easier than ever to design and implement **cutting-edge** embedded systems, and the future looks bright for innovation in this space.

Chapter 25: Building Your First Full Embedded System Project

In this final chapter, we will combine everything you've learned throughout the book to create a **complete embedded system project**. This chapter is designed to give you practical experience in applying the skills and concepts you've acquired to build an embedded system from the ground up, including hardware selection, software design, and system integration.

The focus will be on **home automation**, a highly relevant and real-world application that leverages a variety of embedded system components like **sensors**, **microcontrollers**, **wireless communication**, and **user interfaces**. You will go through the entire design and development process: **requirements gathering**, **component selection**, **programming**, **integration**, and **testing**. By the end of this chapter, you will have developed the confidence to undertake your own embedded system projects.

---

1. *Putting It All Together*
a) Defining the Project Scope:

- Understanding the core objectives of the home automation system.

- Identifying the necessary components: sensors, actuators, microcontroller, power supply, and communication modules.
- Establishing communication protocols: Wi-Fi for remote control, sensors for temperature and motion detection, and actuators for controlling devices.

b) Designing the Hardware:

- **Selecting the Microcontroller**: Choosing the right microcontroller based on required input/output pins, communication interfaces, and power consumption.
- **Sensor Integration**: Connecting and interfacing with sensors like temperature, humidity, and motion detectors.
- **Actuators and Relays**: Wiring actuators (e.g., motors, lights, or relays) to the microcontroller for controlling household appliances.
- **Wireless Modules**: Using Wi-Fi (ESP8266/ESP32) or Bluetooth for communication between the embedded system and a mobile app or cloud platform.

c) Software Development:

- **Writing the Firmware**: Developing the C code to handle sensor readings, process data, and control actuators.

- **Communication Protocols**: Configuring the wireless communication (Wi-Fi/Bluetooth) for sending and receiving data.
- **Real-Time Control**: Using timers and interrupts to manage time-sensitive events, such as turning off a light after a set period.
- **User Interface**: Building a basic user interface (mobile app or web interface) to control the home automation system remotely.

d) Power Management:

- Ensuring that the system operates efficiently and consumes minimal power, especially if it's battery-powered.
- Implementing **sleep modes** to reduce power consumption during idle periods.

---

2. Real-World Example: Building a Home Automation System
a) System Overview:

- The home automation system will allow users to remotely control household devices (e.g., lights, fans) and monitor environmental conditions (e.g., temperature, humidity, motion).

- Users will be able to control the system via a **mobile app** or **web interface** that communicates with the microcontroller over a **Wi-Fi** network.

b) Step-by-Step Development:

1. **System Requirements**:

   ○ **Sensors**: Temperature, humidity, and motion sensors to monitor the environment.

   ○ **Actuators**: Relays to control lights and fans based on sensor data.

   ○ **Microcontroller**: ESP8266/ESP32 for Wi-Fi connectivity and processing.

   ○ **Power Supply**: Adequate for the microcontroller and connected components.

2. **Hardware Setup**:

   ○ **Wiring the Sensors**: Connect the temperature and humidity sensor (e.g., DHT22) to the microcontroller's input pins, ensuring proper power and grounding.

   ○ **Relays and Actuators**: Interface the relays with the microcontroller's GPIO pins to control the switching of household devices (e.g., lights).

   ○ **Wi-Fi Module**: If using ESP8266 or ESP32, ensure correct configuration for Wi-Fi communication.

3. **Software Design**:

- o **Reading Sensors**: Write C code to read sensor values periodically.

- o **Control Logic**: Develop logic to control relays based on sensor input (e.g., turn on the fan if the temperature exceeds a threshold).

- o **Communication with the Cloud**: Send sensor data to a cloud platform (e.g., AWS, Google Firebase) for remote monitoring.

- o **Mobile App/GUI**: Create a simple mobile app or web interface for the user to control the system.

4. **Integration and Testing**:

- o **Integrating Hardware and Software**: Once the firmware is written, load it onto the microcontroller and test the communication with the sensors and relays.

- o **User Interface**: Test the communication between the mobile app/web interface and the microcontroller.

- o **Real-Time Operation**: Test if the system can read sensors, control devices in real-time, and send data over Wi-Fi.

5. **Power Management**: Implement power-saving features like sleep mode for the microcontroller to extend battery life, if needed.

6. **Final Testing**: Thoroughly test all system functionalities to ensure it meets the design requirements, including hardware reliability, software performance, and power consumption.

By the end of this chapter, you will have successfully built a **home automation system**, gaining hands-on experience with microcontroller programming, sensor interfacing, communication protocols, and wireless integration. This project will solidify your understanding of embedded systems and give you a strong foundation for tackling more complex applications in the future.

This comprehensive project will help you develop critical skills in **embedded systems design**, preparing you for real-world embedded development challenges.

4o mini

Chapter 26: Troubleshooting and Optimizing Embedded Systems

In this chapter, we will dive into the critical aspects of **troubleshooting** and **optimizing** embedded systems, two essential skills for any embedded systems engineer. While designing and building embedded systems can be a complex and rewarding experience, ensuring that the system works reliably and efficiently in real-world conditions is equally important. Troubleshooting helps identify and fix bugs and issues, while optimization focuses on improving the system's performance, power consumption, and overall reliability.

This chapter will cover various tools, techniques, and strategies for debugging and optimizing embedded systems. By the end of this chapter, you'll be able to identify problems in your embedded systems and improve their efficiency, leading to more robust and efficient designs.

---

1. Troubleshooting Embedded Systems
a) Identifying Common Issues:

- **Hardware Issues:**
    - Power problems: voltage instability, insufficient current, and improper connections.

- o Interference from external signals or grounding issues.

- **Software Issues:**
  - o Bugs in logic or code that lead to unexpected behavior.
  - o Memory corruption or stack overflows.
  - o Communication failures (e.g., UART, SPI, or I2C).

b) Tools for Troubleshooting:

- **Serial Communication Debugging:**
  - o Using **UART** (Universal Asynchronous Receiver/Transmitter) for serial communication to log data and error messages.
- **In-Circuit Debuggers (ICD):**
  - o Tools like **JTAG** or **SWD (Serial Wire Debug)** that allow you to interact with microcontrollers in real-time, step through your code, and monitor variables.
- **Logic Analyzers and Oscilloscopes:**
  - o Using hardware tools to monitor digital signals and verify timing, communication, and waveform integrity.
- **LED Indicators:**
  - o Using LEDs as simple status indicators to diagnose system states or track specific code execution points.

- **Software Debuggers:**
  - Using built-in debuggers in IDEs (e.g., **Keil uVision**, **MPLAB X**) to perform breakpoints, watch variables, and step through the code.

c) Debugging Tips and Techniques:

- Start by isolating the problem. Is it hardware or software? Is it a power issue, communication error, or logic bug?
- Always check the power supply first. Ensure the voltage levels are appropriate for the microcontroller and peripherals.
- Use simple diagnostic tools such as **serial print statements** or **LED blink patterns** to get quick feedback from your system.
- **Divide and conquer:** If you're having trouble with a complex system, break it down into smaller, more manageable pieces and test each independently.

d) Real-World Example:

- **Debugging a UART Communication Issue:**
  - A microcontroller isn't properly transmitting data over UART. We'll show how to use **serial debugging** to print logs and check whether the issue lies in the software logic, hardware wiring, or baud rate mismatch.

2. *Optimizing Embedded Systems*
a) Optimizing for Performance:

- **Code Efficiency:**
  - o Minimizing instruction cycles by optimizing algorithms and code structure. For instance, using **bitwise operators** to reduce processing time in specific operations.
  - o **Memory usage** optimization: Understanding the limitations of embedded systems, such as **RAM** and **flash memory**, and using them efficiently.
- **Interrupts:**
  - o Minimizing system load by using **interrupts** to handle time-sensitive tasks instead of using polling loops, which can waste processing time.
- **Data Structures:**
  - o Choosing optimal data structures to minimize both **memory usage** and **processing time**. For instance, using **ring buffers** for continuous data flow.

b) Optimizing for Power Consumption:

- **Power Profile Optimization:**
  - o Using low-power modes to reduce the consumption of the microcontroller when it's idle. For example,

using the **sleep** mode and optimizing the duty cycle of **PWM signals**.

- **Efficient Use of Peripherals:**
    - Making use of peripherals such as **timers** or **watchdog timers** to manage time-based activities rather than using the main processor.
- **Dynamic Power Scaling:**
    - Reducing the operating frequency of the microcontroller and scaling down its voltage (Dynamic Voltage and Frequency Scaling, DVFS) when the full processing power is not needed.

c) Optimizing for Reliability:

- **Error Detection and Correction:**
    - Implementing **watchdog timers** to ensure the system doesn't hang indefinitely due to software bugs or crashes.
    - Using **parity bits** or **CRC checks** for communication reliability.
- **Redundancy and Fault Tolerance:**
    - Incorporating redundancy in critical systems (e.g., dual microcontrollers, sensors) to increase system reliability and fault tolerance.

d) Real-World Example:

- **Optimizing an IoT Device for Power Consumption:**
  - An IoT sensor node is running on a battery and needs to last for months. We will walk through the process of reducing power consumption by using **low-power modes**, **sleep cycles**, and careful scheduling of communication with the cloud to ensure minimal power use.

3. Best Practices for Embedded System Optimization

a) Code Quality:

- Writing clean, readable, and modular code to ensure maintainability and easy identification of bottlenecks.
- Using **profiling tools** to analyze code performance and identify critical sections.

b) Continuous Testing:

- Setting up continuous integration (CI) systems to run automated tests on embedded systems to catch performance or memory issues early in the development process.

c) Resource Management:

- **Memory allocation:** Minimize dynamic memory allocation, avoid memory fragmentation, and ensure proper memory deallocation.
- **CPU load management:** Efficient scheduling of tasks, use of interrupts, and balancing processing tasks to avoid bottlenecks in multi-tasking systems.

d) Documentation and Version Control:

- Maintaining comprehensive documentation for the hardware setup, system requirements, and performance considerations.
- Using **version control systems** like **Git** to manage code and hardware changes effectively across multiple developers.

---

4. Real-World Troubleshooting and Optimization Example:
a) The Problem:

- A home automation system controlling lights, heating, and cooling is experiencing intermittent communication issues and high power consumption. The system uses wireless communication and multiple sensors.

b) Troubleshooting Steps:

- First, check if the system is in low-power mode during idle times.
- Use serial output to verify whether the microcontroller is handling interrupts correctly and responding to sensor readings.
- Inspect the UART or SPI communication to ensure there's no data loss or timing issues.

c) Optimization Actions:

- Optimize the sleep cycle of the microcontroller to ensure it stays in low-power mode for the majority of the time.
- Refactor the code to minimize the number of active cycles and use interrupts instead of polling.
- Reduce the number of transmissions or batch sensor data to minimize power usage during wireless communication.

In embedded system development, **troubleshooting** and **optimization** are essential skills that go beyond simply writing functional code. These skills ensure that the system performs well, remains reliable over time, and is as efficient as possible in terms of power consumption, processing speed, and resource management. By understanding how to effectively debug and optimize embedded systems, you will be well-equipped to tackle real-world engineering challenges and develop robust, high-performance embedded solutions.

Chapter 27: Advanced Techniques for Embedded Systems Development

As embedded systems continue to evolve, developers must explore more advanced techniques and methodologies to keep up with increasing system complexity and the demand for better performance, reliability, and scalability. This chapter will explore some of the cutting-edge practices and techniques used by embedded systems engineers in real-world applications.

We'll look at some advanced tools, methodologies, and techniques that can help you push the boundaries of what's possible with embedded systems. From low-level hardware optimization to integrating modern technologies like AI and machine learning into embedded systems, this chapter will help you gain the knowledge and experience needed to develop more sophisticated and powerful embedded systems.

1. Low-Level Optimization Techniques
a) Optimizing for Performance:

- **Code Optimization:**
  - In embedded systems, optimizing for speed and memory is crucial. Learn how to reduce code size

and execution time, which is particularly important for systems with limited resources.

- o Strategies for optimizing loops, conditional branches, and functions.
- o Use of **inline functions** and **macros** for faster execution.
- o Avoiding dynamic memory allocation, especially in real-time systems.

b) Memory Optimization:

- Embedded systems often operate with strict memory constraints, and managing memory efficiently is a key challenge. We'll discuss techniques to optimize both **RAM** and **Flash memory**.
- Memory management strategies:
  - o Memory pools, buffer management, and **stack usage optimization**.
  - o **Static allocation** vs. **dynamic allocation** and when to use each.

c) Optimizing Power Consumption:

- Power optimization is essential for battery-operated embedded systems. Techniques include:
  - o Using **sleep modes** and **low-power modes** for idle components.

- o Optimizing clock speeds and disabling unused peripherals.
- o Efficient **power gating** strategies.

---

2. *Real-Time and Multi-Core Embedded Systems*
a) Real-Time Systems Challenges:

- Real-time systems require meeting strict timing constraints. Learn how to implement and manage **real-time tasks**, manage **interrupts**, and prioritize system functions.
- Design patterns for **predictability** and **time-sensitive operations**.
- Overview of real-time operating systems (RTOS) such as **FreeRTOS** or **Zephyr** and their use in meeting deadlines.

b) Multi-Core Processors:

- **Parallel processing** in embedded systems using multi-core microcontrollers.
- Techniques for dividing tasks across multiple cores for **increased processing power**.
- Synchronization techniques (e.g., semaphores, mutexes) for managing shared resources in multi-core systems.

---

3. Integrating AI and Machine Learning with Embedded Systems
a) Adding Intelligence to Embedded Systems:

- Learn how to integrate AI and machine learning models into embedded systems to enable **decision-making** and **pattern recognition** on the edge.
- **Tiny Machine Learning (TinyML):**
    o A growing field that enables the deployment of machine learning models on microcontrollers with limited processing power and memory.
- Tools and libraries:
    o **TensorFlow Lite** for microcontrollers.
    o Using **edge AI processors** like Google's **Edge TPU** to run models locally.

b) Real-World Example:

- Implementing a **voice recognition** system on a microcontroller to control a smart home device using simple AI algorithms.
- Training models offline and deploying them on embedded systems for tasks such as **predictive maintenance**, **sensor data analysis**, and **gesture recognition**.

---

4. Advanced Peripherals and Interfaces

a) High-Speed Communication Protocols:

- Explore more complex and high-speed communication protocols used in embedded systems, including:
  - **Ethernet** and **TCP/IP** stacks for networked embedded systems.
  - **CAN** (Controller Area Network) and **Modbus** for industrial systems.
  - Advanced **SPI** and **I2C** configurations for faster data exchange.

b) High-Performance Sensors and Actuators:

- Learn how to interface with high-speed and high-resolution sensors and actuators.
- Working with advanced sensors such as **LiDAR**, **IMUs** (Inertial Measurement Units), and **high-frequency cameras**.
- Interfacing with **actuators** like **servo motors**, **linear actuators**, and **piezoelectric systems** for precise control in robotics and automation.

---

5. Security in Advanced Embedded Systems

a) Embedded System Security Threats:

- As embedded systems become more connected, security becomes even more critical. Learn about the potential threats to embedded systems, including:
  - o **Unauthorized access**, **data leakage**, and **device manipulation**.
  - o How to protect your system from attacks like **buffer overflows**, **code injection**, and **side-channel attacks**.

b) Implementing Secure Communication:

- Techniques for ensuring **data integrity** and **confidentiality** in communication:
  - o Using **TLS/SSL** for secure data transmission.
  - o **Public key infrastructure (PKI)** for secure authentication and encryption.
  - o Techniques like **message authentication codes (MAC)** and **digital signatures**.

c) Secure Boot and Firmware Updates:

- Understanding the concept of **secure boot** to ensure that only authenticated and authorized firmware can run on your system.
- Implementing **over-the-air (OTA)** updates with **secure communication** protocols.

6. Advanced Debugging and Diagnostics

a) Debugging Tools for Complex Systems:

- Learn how to use advanced debugging tools and techniques to analyze embedded systems that are not behaving as expected.
  - o **JTAG** and **SWD** (Serial Wire Debug) for low-level debugging.
  - o Analyzing **memory dumps** and **processor registers**.
  - o Using **logic analyzers** and **oscilloscopes** for signal analysis.

b) Performance Profiling and Bottleneck Identification:

- Tools for profiling embedded systems to identify performance bottlenecks:
  - o Using software profilers like **gprof** or **ARM's DS-5** for analyzing system performance.
  - o Identifying CPU and memory usage bottlenecks and optimizing code accordingly.

7. Real-World Project: Designing an Advanced Embedded System

a) Integrating Concepts into a Complex System:

- The culmination of this chapter is a real-world, comprehensive project where you integrate many of the advanced techniques discussed.
- Example project: Designing an **autonomous robot** that integrates high-performance sensors, advanced communication protocols, and real-time processing.

b) Testing and Validation:

- Final testing for performance, reliability, and robustness.
- Techniques for debugging and optimizing the complete system.

By the end of this chapter, you will have gained the skills needed to tackle complex embedded system projects, troubleshoot difficult issues, and optimize your systems for performance, security, and reliability.

www.ingramcontent.com/pod-product-compliance
Lightning Source LLC
LaVergne TN
LVHW051325050326
832903LV00031B/3376